*How To Profit From
Your Personal Computer*

The Hayden Microcomputer Series

Consulting Editor: Ted Lewis, Oregon State University

†Consulting Editor: Sol Libes, Amateur Computer Group of New Jersey and
 Union Technical Institute

How To Profit From
Your Personal Computer

Ted Lewis

HAYDEN BOOK COMPANY, INC.
Rochelle Park, New Jersey

Dedication

They Were There When I Needed Them:

Madeline
Paige
Todd
Lois
Gyle
Alfie
Osckie

Library of Congress Cataloging in Publication Data

Lewis, Theodore Gyle, 1941
   How to profit from your personal computer.

   Includes index.
   1. Miniature computers. 2. Microcomputers.
3. Electronic data processing. I. Title.
QA76.5.L493   658'.05   78-2780
ISBN 0-8104-5761-X

4	5	6	7	8	9	PRINTING

78	79	80	81	82	83	84	85	86	YEAR

PREFACE

My goal in writing this material was to convey the important features of personal computers useful to computer aficionadoes. This includes the ability to select equipment intelligently, to analyze, in global terms, a problem for a business application, hobby, or educational experiment, and to translate problem solutions into real computer systems. Specifically, I hope the reader will learn how to configure a system to fit the needs of an application; to implement that system using the programming techniques I have developed; and to understand the fundamentals of data processing. These fundamentals include file structures, programming structures, and some knowledge of computer hardware structures.

Finally, I have endeavored to produce an enjoyable, readable book that conveys information in an easily understood manner. I hope everyone who reads the following pages will benefit in some degree from the experience.

I want to thank my typist, Ms. Homyer, and my students for their comments. I would also like to thank Capt. Terry Elton, Dave Cautley, and others at Oregon State University who have purposely or inadvertently contributed to this work. Also, many business-related problems were solved for me by Bart Johnson and several programming problems overcome for me by Gerry Barnes, both of General Information Systems, Inc.

The guidance of Pat Terrell of the Portland Byteshop, Dianne Littwin of Hayden Books, and Henry Ledgard of the University of Massachusetts contributed in nonobvious ways to the finished product.

T. G. LEWIS

CONTENTS

Chapter One

BUTTERFLIES AND COMPUTERS ARE FREE

"As a young man I was advised to study Radio because that was supposed to be a field with a future. Perhaps I should have followed the advice, but somehow there just never was time to do it. Now of course, radio and television are big industries. If only I had known what the next 30 years would be like . . . ."

Crackatoah Jones, 1954

What Computing Is Coming To

The LSI Revolution

The American space program may turn out to be a bargain for twentieth-century American taxpayers. New plastics, rare metal alloys, a wealth of basic research, and a military arsenal were the result of billions of dollars spent by NASA. Now, ten years later, it is the American citizen who is benefiting from the by-products of that bygone decade. In fact, it is very possible that personal computers found in many homes, offices, and schools today would never have been possible without the space program and its requirements for miniature, lightweight, and low-powered electronics. Almost certainly, we can say that small computers are "Made in America" because of the money invested in space-age electronics.

Large-scale integrated circuits (LSI) made of metal-oxide-silicon (MOS) transistors are used in constructing personal computers. LSI is a revolutionary technology that makes it possible to put thousands of transistors on a single silicon wafer smaller than a human fingernail. The wafer, packaged inside a dual-inline-package (DIP) of ceramic and copper, is sold as a single circuit called a "chip."

The computer industry is being revolutionized by chip circuits that are sophisticated enough to perform the functions of a complete computer. These innovative chips are able to add, test, compare, and move numbers from one place to another. They can be combined with other chips designed to store data. When storage chips are added,

1

we have the essential ingredients for a powerful computer. A *micro-computer* is a DIP chip set containing a processor chip (the *microprocessor*), at least one memory chip (the *memory*), and other chips that perform input and output, timing (the *clock*), and other functions that we will learn about later.

Surprisingly, computers are much less expensive than the devices needed to communicate with them. These devices, called *peripherals*, include keyboards, printers, and large-storage devices such as disk and tape. A keyboard/screen combination is usually available for input to the computer, and a line printer is usually used to output reports from the computer. Disk and tape devices are often needed to hold data until they are required by the computer. We will discuss the merits as well as problems associated with each one of these devices.

Since LSI technology has reduced the size and cost of computers as well as the power they require, old ideas about computers have been disappearing. Here are some of the old ideas, versus some of the new ideas ("old" means before 1970):

The Monolith Myth
  Computers are large, costly, and complicated and should thus be run by corporations that need large, expensive machines.
versus
  Computers are small, inexpensive, and simple and thus can be run by anyone interested in solving domestic problems or playing games, or anyone considering himself a computer aficionado.

The Hands-Off Myth
  Since computers are expensive, they should be centralized, and users should have access to them only by means of remote stations connected to telephones.
versus
  Computers are available to everyone and should thus be decentralized and distributed to anyone who needs one. Access should be hands-on.

These two myths are only samples of outmoded ideas about computers. The end result of modern thinking about computers is home computers, or what we call *personal computers*. What exactly is behind the development called *personal computing?*

A typical home computer, or businessman's personal computer, as shown in Fig. 1.1, represents the ultimate achievement in electronics. It is inexpensive, small, powerful, and extremely useful. Furthermore, small personal computers of this kind are environmentally safe, require little electrical power and no special chemicals or pollutants, and are constructed by relatively clean manufacturing processes. How did such

Fig. 1.1 A personal computer consisting of a processor, input keyboard/CRT, line printer, and diskette (*Courtesy*, Madeline Rubin)

technical masterpieces come about? The answer to this question is part of the LSI revolution.

Hardware Slang

The nickname "MOS" is derived from the manufacturing process that uses a combination of a Metal gate, Oxide insulation film, and Silicon base. An MOS is illustrated by the "transistor" of Fig. 1.2. A transistor acts as a very simple switch much like the light switch found in most homes. When power is turned "on" at the metal gate, the transistor is turned "off" (no current flows from A to B), and when the power is turned "off" at the metal gate, the current at A is allowed to flow to B.

How transistors work provides a deep lesson in solid-state physics. Briefly, we can understand the transistor of Fig. 1.2 as follows. The silicon dioxide base contains many negative charges (surplus of electrons), while the channels engraved in the silicon dioxide base contain many positive charges (shortage of electrons). When potential is applied at the metal gate, either current is encouraged to flow from one channel to the next, or a field is created that repels the flow from one channel to the next. Thus a transistor is a switch that controls the flow of current.

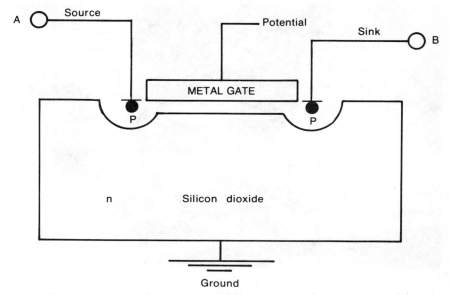

Fig. 1.2 A transistor as a p-MOS device

The transistor of Fig. 1.2 is called a *p-MOS device* because the channels are engraved and filled with positively charged metal. The transistor could also be engraved and filled with a negatively charged metal, in which case it would be called an *n-MOS device*.

In Fig. 1.3(A) we see how combining an n-MOS with a p-MOS device leads to a complementary MOS (called a *CMOS*). A CMOS is of higher speed than a MOS but more costly to build. Also, in Fig. 1.3(B), we illustrate the idea behind a bipolar MOS, which is a technology that yields very high speeds. Other technologies are possible; for example, a VMOS involves a technology that is low-cost and yields high speeds because of the simplicity of a V-shaped transistor. VMOS is used mainly to construct memory.

In either technique, the transistors produced from MOS technology are reduced in size so that thousands of them might be constructed on the head of a pin. This process is called *masking* and requires a very controlled environment (maximally clean room) because of the possible impurities that might ruin the circuit.

The *mask* is actually a diagram of the transistors, connecting lines, and other electronic parts needed to construct memory, processors, and special-purpose computer parts. The mask diagram is photographed, and the photograph shrunk so that it becomes a very small "picture" of the mask. The reduced picture is then etched onto the silicon base by a photochemical process related to film developing.

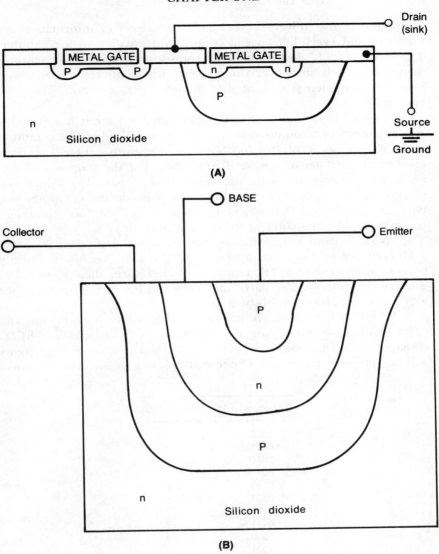

Fig. 1.3 (A) A CMOS device, and (B) bipolar geometry for a transistor

This process of photo reduction is the secret to the MOS miniaturization that we call LSI technology.

The MOS devices shown in Figs. 1.2 and 1.3 are glorified switches. When turned "on" or "off," they *represent* a single unit of information. The fundamental unit of information, therefore, is the answer "yes" or "no." In the same way that atoms are used to build every known compound in the universe, "yes" and "no" pieces of information are used to build every known collection of information in a computer. The "on" and "off" feature of MOS transistors fit computing requirements very nicely since everything stored in a computer can be coded into the fundamental unit of information, "yes" or "no." This unit has a name; a *bit*.

A bit of information is sometimes called a *mark* if it represents an "on," or "yes," condition; it is said to be *cleared* if the condition of the MOS device is "off," or "no." Other names given to these conditions are *true* or *false, one* or *zero*, and *set* or *reset*. For the purposes of this book, we will consider a bit of information to have the values one or zero. This means that everything stored inside the computer will be either a "1" or a "0," which represent a "yes" or "no" condition, respectively, of a transistor or group of transistors.

As an illustration, suppose we want to store the number "5" inside a MOS-device personal computer. The "5" cannot be stored directly because it is neither a "1" nor a "0." Therefore, the "5" must be decomposed into smaller parts, and each smaller part must be either a "1" or a "0." How can this be done?

In Fig. 1.4, we have constructed a table of bits to show one way to *encode* digits by putting together many bits. This code, called "BCD" (Binary Coded Decimal), is the simplest method of storing single digits within computer memories. Other methods are possible, and we will

Bit encoding	Decimal digit
0000	0
0001	1
0010	2
0011	3
0100	4
0101	5
0110	6
0111	7
1000	8
1001	9

Fig. 1.4 The BCD code for digits

study them when the need arises. Notice in Fig. 1.4 the four bits used to store the number "5." Thus, inside the computer's memory, the MOS switches will be set to 0101, meaning the decimal digit "5."

Fortunately, personal computers are designed so that their users rarely need to know which bits are set, how many bits are needed to store any particular number, or even that the memory is made up of MOS transistors. It is useful to know many of the words used by computer people, however, when buying a computer or talking to a programmer. For this reason, we will often explain the current meanings associated with common computer slang. A complete glossary of computer slang is provided in the Appendix for quick reference.

Anatomy of a Personal Computer

Every computer has at least four parts: (1) the processor, (2) main memory, (3) input control, and (4) output control. In Fig. 1.5, we see pictures of typical hardware for each of these functions.

The processor controls the entire system. It is the processor that performs addition of numbers, conversion of characters to numbers or numbers to characters, and other "intelligent" functions. For example, suppose that we wanted a personal computer to update the balance of a checkbook. The processor would subtract the amount of the last check from the current balance and produce a new balance. Suppose that the current balance is $105.50 and the amount of the check, $23.35. The processor would perform subtraction to obtain $82.15.

Before the processor could perform the intended subtraction, however, it would request the number "105.50" from the input device. To obtain it, if the input device is a keyboard, a human being must strike the keyboard. Finally, the processor would cause the answer of "82.15" to be displayed by commanding the output device to print "8," "2," ".", "1," and "5."

The processor must be told what steps to take in a way similar to teaching a small child. Suppose that a child's parent wants the child to bring him a drink of water. If the child is old enough, the parent merely has to say, "Please bring me a glass of water." If the child is younger, the parent must be more specific and say, "Please, go into the kitchen, get a glass from the cupboard, pour water into the glass, and bring it to me." Furthermore, if the child is very young, the adult may have to give extremely detailed instructions. In fact, the parent may need to show the child by walking through the door, turning right, walking to the cupboard, opening the cupboard door, reaching for a glass, and so forth.

Unfortunately, the intelligence of a MOS personal computer is much like that of a very young child. In order to make the processor do what we want, we must specify very detailed instructions for it. These detailed instructions are called *machine-language instructions.* Furthermore, since the machine language instructions are taken from main memory one at a time, they must be encoded into "yes" and

Fig. 1.5 BYTE shop processor, main memory, input terminal, and output printer (*Courtesy*, Madeline Rubin)

"no" bit patterns. Each one of these bit patterns is called a *machine instruction.*

As a quick illustration of machine language, the table of Fig. 1.6 lists a few functions that most personal computers can perform. Notice that each instruction contains only eight ones and zeros. The pattern

Machine language bit pattern for function	Function performed
1000 0101	Addition
0110 1111	Copy data
1100 1010	Skip next instruction
1111 1110	Compare
0000 1111	Shift

Fig. 1.6 Machine language of the author's personal computer

of eight bits for each function is stored in main memory until needed by the processor.

Fortunately, it is also possible to give instructions to a personal computer at a more sophisticated level. In fact, we can instruct a computer to "get me a drink of water" on a level of intelligence similar to that of an older child. This is possible if the personal computer comes equipped with a built-in machine-language program memory that increases its level of intelligence to that of an older child. In this case, the personal computer's processor is able to communicate in a *higher-level language*. The high-level language that is used in this book is called *BASIC*. We will return to a discussion of BASIC later.

Memory

The memory of a personal computer is usually made up of many different kinds of devices. For example, a ROM (Read-Only Memory) is used to increase the personal computer's intelligence to the level of BASIC or some other language. Since this memory never needs to be altered once the bit patterns are recorded, it is made read-only. ROM also has an advantage over other MOS devices: It cannot be altered even when the computer is unplugged. Since normal MOS reverts to all "yes" conditions when the power is removed, it is called *volatile*. Since ROM is nonvolatile, it provides a very good memory for storing instructions that must never be "forgotten."

Most of the main memory is *read and write* memory. Computer people call this memory *RAM* (Random-Access Memory) because it is used for storing both instructions and data that must be fetched at random intervals and at random locations within itself. We can better understand memory and how it works by comparing it to a postal service.

Suppose that mailman Jones has one thousand letters to deliver. He must know the address of each letter, and he must know how to get to each mailbox along his route. Thus, each mailbox is known by its address. The computer memory works in the same way. Each "mailbox" in RAM or ROM has an address associated with it. When a "letter" is delivered, the "mailbox" is "found" by searching along the "route" until its exact location has been reached.

The "mailboxes" of computer memory are of various sizes. The smallest mailboxes contain eight bits each. Groups of eight bits are called *bytes*. Several (two, four) bytes are typically combined to form a *word*. Often *words* are grouped together into *arrays* of words. An *array* may consist of one, two, or a thousand words.

Each byte of a personal computer has an address. The address will be a number between zero and the *size* of memory. For example, 400 is the location or address of an eight-bit byte that is 401 bytes from the beginning of memory. (Remember that the first byte has address 000).

Main memory is relatively expensive and can be purchased in small or large sizes. The sizes vary in powers of two; for example, 1024 (2^{10}) is known as 1K (pronounced "one-kay") of memory. "Two-kay" of memory, 2K, has a capacity of 2048 bytes. Thus, "K" is shorthand for 1024 bytes. Often the unit of measure "KB" (kilo-bytes) is used in place of "K" to distinguish between bytes and words. A typical personal computer has 16K of RAM memory.

Input /Output

The input and output control portions of a personal computer handle a variety of peripherals. Typically, they consist of a keyboard /screen (CRT) and printer, but there may also be devices like a card reader or a telephone.

Since all data stored inside the main memory is encoded in patterns of ones and zeros, a problem arises in communicating to human beings via an input terminal or a line printer. This problem was disclosed briefly by Fig. 1.4, where BCD (Binary Coded Decimal) was used to encode digits. What can be done to encode alphabetic and special characters?

The ASCII code is used by personal computers to translate alphanumeric (alphabetic and numeric) data into bit patterns and back again. ASCII, which stands for American Standard Code for Information Interchange, is one of the many accepted codes in use.

Each ASCII byte has seven or eight bits. Each bit, remember, is representative of a transistor condition. We can convert from characters to bits and vice versa by consulting the table of Fig. 1.7. Actually, it is not necessary to perform the translation by hand because conversion is the function of the input /output control portion of personal computers. The input /output devices, along with the processor, perform ASCII

ASCII character	Bit pattern	Decimal number
A	0100 0001	65
B	0100 0010	66
C	0100 0011	67
1	0011 0001	49
2	0011 0010	50
3	0011 0011	51
$	0010 0100	36
=	0011 1101	61

Fig. 1.7 ASCII Codes for some characters found on the keyboard

code conversion. The conversion, in turn, guarantees that the proper bit pattern is stored in memory.

The ASCII code for the letter "C" is revealed in Fig. 1.7 as "0100 0011" in binary. This means that a pattern of "yes" and "no" conditions are set within the MOS memory of a personal computer containing the letter "C." The input/output devices connected to the personal computer interpret the binary pattern as a command to display "C," when in reality the information comprising the letter "C" is the bit pattern chosen for ASCII encoding.

The four parts of a personal computer are components made from semiconductor circuits, cables, metal, and glass. This is only half of the story, however, because hardware is useless unless accompanied by the necessary *control*. The control part of a computer is called *software* and *firmware*.

Firmware is any program or collection of programs stored in ROM (Read-Only-Memory). The term is derived from the firmness of ROM storage, in order to distinguish such control from software control.

As an example of this control, the personal computer shown in Fig. 1.1 contains a small amount of ROM used to store firmware. The control provided by this firmware allows a user to start the computer easily without having to enter patterns of bits (machine language) manually. This feature is called *autoloading*, or firmware *bootstrapping*.

Software is any program or collection of programs (temporarily) stored in MOS RAM. The processor will perform only those functions that are coded in bit patterns and stored in ROM or RAM. The bit patterns are stored one after the other, beginning at some location specified by the programmer and ending with the last control pattern. Each bit pattern occupies a word of memory and is called a *machine instruction*.

The machine instructions comprising a program are *loaded* into RAM by another program called the *loader*. The program is then *executed* or *run* to carry out the intended operations on the data which is also loaded into RAM.

The beginning of a program is called its *load point* in memory. The address of the first instruction executed is called the *entry point* of the program. Every program is loaded in memory at its *load point* and executed beginning at its *entry point.*

Software is generally subdivided into parts or types of programs that differ according to their control functions. *System software* is the collection of programs provided by the computer manufacturer; it is intended to help a user write other programs. Examples of system software are higher-level languages, editor programs, and programs to guide the execution of other programs. An *operating system* is a firmware or software program that controls the execution of all other programs in the personal computer. For example, the operating system controls the interaction between the user, the editor, and the BASIC language interpreter.

Applications software is the collection of programs needed to control the problem solving and data processing capability of a computer. Examples of applications software are Payroll, Accounts Receivables, and General Ledger programs. The methods and uses of computers in applications programming make up the central subject of this book. With this brief background in computer systems terminology, we hope the subjects of computer selection, programming applications, and methods for getting the most from your personal computer may be clearly explained in the sections to follow.

Computer Tycoons and You

The LSI revolution has lowered the entry fee for computing as a hobby, business, or science. In the past, it was only business tycoons or universities who could think of owning a computer system. Now it is only the lack of knowledge and not money that is the barrier to owning your own computer. In fact, the basic premise of this book is boxed below.

Only lack of knowledge and lack of an awareness of the usefulness of computers are barriers to anyone wanting a personal computer.

Since the author believes that this premise is true, it is the purpose of this book to explain how personal computers operate and show you how to apply them to commonly encountered situations. You may never want to become a professional programmer, but you can understand what a programmer does. You may never fix a computer, but you may (very soon) purchase a personal computer for your home, school, office, or professional practice. Whatever your situation, this book is a place to start understanding and become aware of what personal computers can do.

A personal computer is a not-so-intelligent being that responds to human beings in a two-way dialogue. This form of dialogue has not always been the way with computers. A *batch system*, for example, is typically a card input/paper output system that processes the data punched into input cards and prints results on output paper. We rarely come into contact with a batch computer. Paychecks are processed once a week and bills are printed once a month on batch computers. There is little interaction other than during "feeding" time and when the results are returned.

A *time-sharing system* is a computer system that combines a centrally located computer with telephone services. The "yes" and "no" bit patterns of information stored in the computer are converted into sounds (a high or low tone) by a device called a *modem* (short for *modulator/demodulator*). The modem works together with an acoustic coupler (mechanical ears that hold the telephone) to transmit the converted sound to or from you, from or to the computer.

Time-sharing works like stereophonic records or tape players. A short burst of sound is sent through the left speaker while the right speaker is silent. Then the reverse happens: A short burst of sound is sent through the right speaker while the left one is silent. This ping-pong action happens at high speed, and the effect is as if both speakers are continuously receiving sound signals. Actually, the alternate sound signals are combined into separate left-side and right-side signals by the stereo before being passed on to the left and right speakers.

Another way to look at time-sharing is to compare the signals to boxcars in a long train. Suppose that the boxcars are numbered 1, 2, 3, 4, ... Furthermore, suppose that boxcars 1, 4, 7, 10, . . . are sent to factory A, while boxcars 2, 5, 8, 11, . . . are sent to factory B. The remaining boxcars numbered 3, 6, 9, 12, . . . are sent to factory C. We might say that the boxcars are time-sharing the railroad because they are actually destined for different factories and yet the same train is transferring them. Finally, imagine a train that travels nearly at the speed of light, and you can see why each factory may think that three separate trains have been used to deliver the boxcars.

A time-shared computer system depends upon very fast processors to give the appearance of being many processors instead of one. When several telephone lines are connected to different terminals, each user may imagine that only he is using the computer.

Unfortunately, there are many drawbacks to time-shared and batch systems. The main ones are as follows:

1. Complexity
2. Data jeopardy
3. The telephone company

In order for a time-sharing system to separate each user's programs and data, elaborate techniques must be used, thus escalating the complexity of the system for both user and computer manufacturer. The user must learn an extravagant amount of computer jargon and procedures. The computer itself must be larger and more costly.

Time-sharing was invented (in the early sixties) to amortize the cost of hardware. At the time, it was a good idea because hardware was the major cost item within the total system. Now, after widespread use, time-sharing has lost its reason for being since hardware is no longer the high cost item it was. Hence, the computer tycoons are now readjusting their thinking about centralized time-shared systems. Instead, they are learning the virtues of personal computers, and there is a movement toward *dispersed systems.*

The question of data jeopardy arises when a time-shared computer is used. Since your own data resides in the central computer along with that of possibly hundreds of other users, it is very likely that you may lose it accidentally or that some unauthorized user will be able to change it. For example, if you store a mailing list in a time-shared computer, and your competitor also uses the same computer, what is to prevent him from getting your mailing list if he is devious enough to want to do so.

Sometimes it is necessary to give access to your data to many users. For example, suppose a company stores personnel files in a time-shared computer. The payroll and personnel departments may both have good reasons to access this file. Special precautions therefore have to be enforced to avoid conflicts in data access. Such a problem of multiple access and infringement upon data is common enough in time-shared systems to have been given a name: the *semaphore problem.*

The semaphore problem is solved by special methods of programming not needed in the dispersed processing world of personal computers. Semaphores may be needed when data is to be purposely shared. In this case, software designers must consider semaphores even for personal computers if they are to be used to access a shared storage device.

The telephone company offers a third reason to avoid time-sharing. Computers and telephones are reliable electronic systems, but they do fail once in a while. A central time-sharing system becomes disabled whenever the telephone fails or one of the users causes the central system to "crash." A system crash is a failure which is severe enough to require a restart of every program in the computer. Restarts often mean hours of delay and may be very costly to users if their data is lost during the restart.

Computer tycoons have controlled batch and time-shared computers for nearly all of the computer's existence. Now, however, the tide is shifting to dispersed computing and you personally. In the next chapter, we will consider how a knowledge of software can help you realize the potential of low-cost, powerful personal computer hardware. Combining a knowledge of software capabilities with an awareness of hardware capabilities will lead to a profitable computer investment. Such knowledge is what made computer tycoons of the past successful, and with personal computers almost anyone who takes time to learn basic concepts can profit too. The age of the *common computer* is what computing is coming to.

Before plunging into details of programming and explanations of how to use a personal computer, we shall study two examples of your way along the yellow brick road to the local computer store.

Chapter Two

ADVENTURES OF TOM SWIFT

AND DR. GOODE

The sky glittered in shades of blue incandescence before them as their raft drifted down the lazy river. What a big world it was for such small boys to be exploring, and yet the chirping birds and buzzing insects seemed to be coaxing them on.

Tom turned to Goode and said, "Bet ya we find treasure round the next bend."

Nothing could harm them. They were indestructible.

The Case of Tom Swift's Motorcycle Shop

RULE: INVENTORY EXPANDS TO FILL WAREHOUSE

Tom Swift always enjoyed mechanical devices. When he was twelve years old, he received a go-cart from his father. They spent hours in the garage building faster and faster versions of the "Streak" as they called it.

When Tom finished high school, he joined the army and happily spent two years repairing trucks. That was an education Tom put to use when he returned home and opened a little garage of his own. He wasn't getting rich, but he was doing okay when he met Jeff Jones.* Jeff was a few years younger than Tom but grew up in the same small town. Jeff came into Tom's shop one day to ask if Tom could fix his motorcycle. It was the first time Tom had ever seen a Japanese motorcyle.

Tom fixed it all right, and before the day was over Tom and Jeff became friends. Tom was fascinated by the bike, and Jeff couldn't believe how expert Tom was as a mechanic. It occurred to Jeff that the two of them made a good team, and after a few drinks at Tom's house that evening they invented Tom Swift's Motorcycle Shop.

*Son of the Crackatoah Jones of Chap. 1.

Jeff sold Japanese motorcycles out front, and Tom repaired them in the back. The business was an immediate success with about half a dozen bikes being sold each week, and more repair business than Tom could handle. In a few years, Jeff and Tom found themselves running a small business with five employees and a sales volume that made them respected businessmen in Podunk Junction.

What Tom and Jeff soon learned about successful small enterprises was a simple fact of business: Inventory expands to fill the warehouse. Since each delivered motorcycle came with a dozen options and a half-dozen colors and sizes, their operation required a stock of hundreds of bikes. In addition, each bike had to be paid for within 30 days of delivery whether Jeff was able to sell it or not. This meant that during any one month, Tom's Motorcycle Shop could be floating hundreds of thousands of dollars in investment.

Another aspect of the business not clearly understood by Tom at the time Jeff convinced him to go into it was the problem associated with spare parts. Every bike sold eventually came back to be repaired or tuned. This meant that Tom's shop also had to stock hundreds of parts in various sizes and models. The stockpile was growing faster than the business, and to make matters worse, each one had a number instead of a name. Tom hopelessly attempted to remember the numbers, but as inventory grew, he became more and more confused.

Problem: How to Minimize Overhead, Maximize Service

Tom and Jeff didn't realize it at first, but they began to lose customers. Whenever Tom became involved in mechanical work, the parts man would interrupt him to ask where the Widget 88 shrewp could be found. The office manager interrupted him to ask about a billing problem or a part number, and the line of people waiting to buy parts grew while work halted. To put it bluntly, service at Tom's Motorcycle Shop was poor. Jeff spent more of his time straightening out invoices and filling out orders for parts and new bikes than he spent selling.

Tom and Jeff were also unhappy because they weren't making as much money as in the past although they were working 14 hours a day. Overwork was ruining their fun, and accountants, lawyers, and the tax man were getting most of their money. What Tom and Jeff wanted to know was, "How can we minimize overhead costs while maximizing customer service and personal attention?"

After Jeff suggested that they hire part-time help, two new assistants joined the staff. A few months later, two more new assistants joined the staff. Soon, Tom and Jeff realized that they would have to hire someone to manage the new assistants, train them, and help out when one of them became ill. It also became evident that the assistants' salaries were outstripping the income derived from the business. Adding new employees was not the answer.

Tom and Jeff were frustrated. Then Tom noticed an ad in the *Podunk Junction Tribune*: "Grand Opening: Computer Shop." The advertisement said anyone could afford a computer to play games, handle payroll, and most important to Tom, manage inventory. Excitedly, Tom called Jeff on the telephone and asked if he had heard about the new computer store.

"Sure," said Jeff, "but we can't afford a computer, and if we could, who would run it?" Jeff had fallen for the "Monolith Myth."

"It says here that anyone can afford one, and that programs for inventory are provided by companies that specialize in small computers," responded Tom. "I think it would be fun to take a look anyway, Jeff," he continued.

"Well, okay, Tom, but what do we know about computers?" Jeff said, rephrasing the "Hands-Off Myth." "Computers are fancy machines and we can't even use a typewriter."

"This ad says they have books explaining how to use the computer, and besides, we taught ourselves how to run a business, didn't we?" countered Tom. "I don't think computers are more complicated than Japanese motorcycle engines, Jeff, and I learned how to put them together without going to Japan."

"If you say so, Tom," Jeff gave in. "I'll pick you up in the morning and we can drop by the computer shop on our way to work. I have to hurry on in, though. We have a bill from the last bike shipment that doesn't match the order I sent in. At least I don't think we ordered five X-22 Swizzles." Jeff sighed and hung up.

Solution: The Inventory Computer

Tom's Motorcycle Shop is confronted with a problem common to thousands of small businesses that deal with parts inventory. Such businesses may be financially sound and have a good product. In fact, it is because of their resounding success that inventory expands beyond their capability to cope with it.

If Tom and Jeff were managing a large corporation, they could buy time on a computer already owned by the company. Chances are, their inventory problem would require only a few minutes processing each day on the computer. If they were to turn to a local timesharing service, they would face the hazards of data jeopardy, unnecessary complexity, and the telephone company. Since Tom and Jeff don't want to lose complete control of their company, their best solution is a special-purpose computer: the inventory computer.

Tom and Jeff decide to turn a personal computer into an inventory computer. This means that they must buy the right hardware and either buy or develop the right software. But before buying anything, they must define exactly what their problem is and identify what it is they want the personal computer to do.

Tom and Jeff must turn to a *systems analyst* or become systems analysts themselves. A systems analyst evaluates the current procedures and determines if a computer can be of value. If it can, the analyst will describe how the use of a computer will benefit the business. Finally, this description can be used to design the computer programs and forms that are needed to carry out his recommendations.

In the case of Tom Swift's Motorcycle Shop, the bottleneck is inventory and the general level of effort needed to order new parts and retrieve them when needed. Tom and Jeff view this problem as a system like that shown in Fig. 2-1.

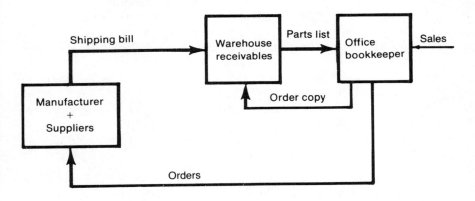

Fig. 2.1 Tom Swift's Motorcycle Shop inventory system

In Tom Swift's Motorcycle Shop inventory system, a parts list is sent from the warehouse to the bookkeeper in the office. The bookkeeper gives a copy to Jeff so that he can aim his salespeople toward reducing the stockpile of new bikes. The bookkeeper also gives a copy to Tom so that he will know what replacement parts are available. Tom uses this list to locate spare parts when needed. In both cases, Tom and Jeff give sales information to the bookkeeper so that new orders can be placed. The new orders must be placed several weeks before the shipping date because there is always a delay in shipment. Hence, since the sales information is always a prediction instead of a precise appraisal of sales, the warehouse will often be overflowing with parts that cannot be sold because of an incorrectly estimated demand. It also means a loss of operating money because, whether the inventory is sold or not, Tom and Jeff must pay for it within 30 days of delivery.

The orders are mailed to various suppliers, and a copy is given to Joe in the warehouse. When Joe receives a new shipment, he checks it with a red pencil on his order copy. When the new shipment is inventoried and stored in the warehouse, Joe writes its part number, description, and location on the parts list, and this goes to the bookkeeper in the office. The bookkeeper pays the bills and reorders all parts that fail to arrive.

The suppliers receive orders and send shipments of parts along with an invoice or bill to the Motorcycle Shop. Each supplier has a problem similar to Tom and Jeff's problem, but their problem will be left to another chapter.

The inventory computer that Tom and Jeff dream about would do the following:

1. Give Tom, Jeff, Joe, and the bookkeeper a daily updated parts list showing in alphabetical or numerical order the (a) part number, (b) part description, (c) part location in the warehouse, and (d) miscellaneous information like supplier's name, unit cost, and quantity on hand.
2. Automatically print orders for new parts whenever the inventory quantity decreases to a given level.
3. Update the inventory lists at the close of each day to show the sales, received shipments, and total value of the inventory.
4. Give Tom, Jeff, Joe, and the bookkeeper (whose name is Carl, but everyone calls him Slim) a day off.

With these goals and desires in mind, Tom and Jeff look forward to visiting the computer shop. What they find there and how they can take advantage of it still lies ahead, but before taking that step, we will look at another problem similar to Tom and Jeff's but also of interest.

Doctor Goode's Growing Practice

RULE: PATIENT BILLINGS EXPAND TO FILL CLINIC

His hard work and sacrifice paid off, because the day after John Goode received his medical degree he was on an airplane to New York to accept an internship in a neighborhood hospital. Later John and his family moved to the Midwest where he opened a GP office in a quiet Kansas town of 100,000 people.

When the Goode's son, Jacob Elan, was thirteen, he had threatened to run off with a band of rock musicians, but he survived those days. More recently, J. E. had become interested in supernatural phenomena and was deep into warlock techniques. He was also a member of a high school computer club.

John and his wife Sue Anne were superb physicians. Their practice grew beyond their ability to cope, and within a few years, they had increased the size of their clinic to five physicians and three office people. Sue Anne was a big' help, but her specialty was surgery, and she spent a lot of time at the community medical center. This left her husband with a management problem: "Patient billing and insurance forms expand to fill the clinic."

Instead of practicing medicine, Dr. Goode spent most of his time correcting statements, assisting the office staff with billing and insurance forms, and scheduling patients. His clinic was always running low of one medicine and overstocked with another. Though it was doing a fantastic business, John was alarmed to find out that during the previous three months over $10,000 in bills had gone unpaid. Upon further investigation, John learned that he lost over $25,000 each year in unpaid bills. These past due accounts were never collected because by the time the office staff discovered them, the patient had moved or died. Simply stated, Doctor Goode's Clinic was not keeping on top of business.

Problem: How to Minimize Cost, Maximize Service

John Goode realized that he faced another challenge in his career: how to minimize cost and at the same time render professional service to his patients. He mentioned this to his son one day after a tiring day arguing with Margie (one of the office staff members). J. E. was working on a science project to compute pi to 300 digits of accuracy with the high school minicomputer.

When John mentioned his problem to J. E., it never occurred to him that personal computing was the answer. J. E. saw the potential benefit immediately, however.

"Why don't you let me write a program to do billing on the school mini? It should be easy enough to do, dad."

"Hey, you may have something there, son!" John's voice had a hint of enthusiasm in it. "I spent all those hours in medical school using computers, and yet never thought of using them in my practice."

"You know, Fred Rotund and I are working on a program now that computes pi to 300 decimal digits," said J. E.. "We use the mini at school every Saturday. Why don't you come along next weekend and watch?"

The next day at the clinic, John brought the subject of computerized billing to the attention of his associates. The idea seemed a little risky to most of them, but the nose and throat man, Jenkins, knew of a batch system service from Des Moines that another local clinic used. Jenkins said that the Henderson Clinic sent their charge slips to the Des Moines computer service by mail and every Tuesday morning they received a print-out and statements to be mailed to each patient billed.

Unknowingly, Dr. Jenkins had fallen for the "Hands-Off Myth." At the time, however, since it seemed like a good idea, they called Henderson Clinic for more information. To their disappointment, the staff at the Henderson Clinic had few good words to say about the Des Moines computer service. The batch system suffered from all forms of batch and time-sharing system drawbacks, among them the following:

1. *Complexity*:   Each patient billing required an office person to fill out a computer card with code numbers and special information. The error rate was very high, and errors went undetected for as long as 30 days. Once an error was discovered, it took 60 days to correct.

2. *Data jeopardy*:   The computer service accidentally erased Henderson Clinic's master file of patients back in September. The office staff had to work overtime in October to reproduce the master file information from old records. The result was a two-month delay in the September billing. By January the mess was straightened out, but not without much suffering.

3. *Postal service difficulties*: In most cases the Henderson records were updated weekly. This meant that current balances on each patient's account were a week out-of-date. Periodically, the mail was late (on one occasion it was even lost in a fire), and the records fell even further behind. Whatever its reliability, the entire clinic's operation depended upon the mail. Needless to say, the bills sent out near Christmas always arrived late.

Dr. Goode and his associates were very disappointed when the Henderson Clinic report was presented at the next staff meeting. At a loss, John dutifully followed his son to school the next Saturday to learn about small computers.

Solution: The Billing Computer

Dr. Goode had come to realize that the answer was a billing computer, but he was still uncertain about the question. "Is it possible to have a computer that stores the names of each patient in its memory somehow, and then at the end of the month to push a button and out come the monthly statements? What does personal computing do to my practice, and do I have to change the way I do things?" These were some of the questions, but he was unsure how they related to his own clinic. He turned to his son J. E. for some answers.

J. E. spent a day in his father's clinic. He watched what went on in the office and asked questions. When the day was over, he came up with the system shown in Fig. 2.2.

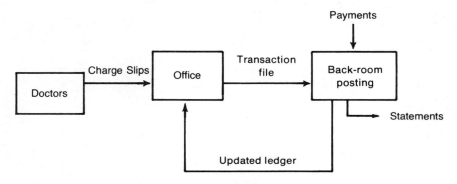

Fig. 2.2 Dr. Goode's Medical Clinic system

Each doctor produces a single charge slip each time he sees a patient. The charge slip is a record of the diagnosis, treatment, and drugs administered during one visit to the clinic.

The completed charge slips are collected at the end of each day, sorted into the correct order, and passed on to the back-room staff. In the back room, the bundle of charge slips is combined with incoming payments and then both payments and charges are posted against the ledger. Each ledger contains every patient's name, address, telephone number, and a list of previous charges and payments. Posting is the process of adding new payments and charges to the list and computing the current balance.

If the current balance is greater than zero, a statement is typed-up and mailed to the patient. If a balance is long overdue (*aged account*), the patient is called by telephone and asked to pay his bill.

A copy of the updated ledger is returned to the main office. This copy is used to answer questions from patients about correct billing, outstanding balance due, and treatment.

The system designed by J. E. was explained to his father and the other physicians at the clinic to give them a better idea of their needs. It then became clear that the following services should be provided by a computer:

1. Storage of all ledger information, containing patient's name, address, telephone number, and outstanding (current) balance.
2. Storage of all transactions pending (not yet posted against ledger).
3. Posting of the transaction file against the ledger and printing of the statements. Preferably each statement is printed in a mailer, with name and address also printed by the computer.
4. Producing an updated ledger listing for use by the staff. This listing can be stored in the computer and queried whenever the information is needed.
5. Producing a summary report for each doctor that will tell him the status of his practice.

With these goals and desires in mind, John and his son J. E. look forward to visiting the computer shop.

Chapter Three

Tom Swift and Dr. Goode Go Shopping

Everything Is Simple Once You Understand It!
Graffito on the north wall

The Computer Store

In the thirties and forties it was refrigerators, radios, and indoor plumbing; in the fifties it was television, hi-fi, and tape recorders; in the sixties it was stereophonic sound, transistorized radios, and color television; in the seventies it is video TV, microwave ovens, quadraphonic sound, and CB radios. In the eighties it will be personal computers, electronic banking, automated kitchens, and microcomputer-controlled consumer appliances like "intelligent" refrigerators, clocks, stoves, heating/cooling systems, and, of course, TV games.

These "gadgets" are coming in the next few years because of the "dollar-volume force" that pushes new technology into new applications. As the cost of an invention is reduced, the demand for it increases. As the demand increases, the unit cost reduces to the extent that demand is stimulated. Technology progresses ever more rapidly as innovations, reduced costs, and increased volumes create ever larger increases in dollar sales. For example, pocket calculators originally sold for $400. Within two years of their introduction as an engineer's tool, the demand for them so increased the dollar-volume sales that the unit cost was driven down to one-tenth of the original figure. The original engineer's tool had been adopted by housewives, students, businessmen, and nearly everyone who could push a button. The expanding market stimulated new innovations not only in such calculators but also in microwave ovens and other electronic implements.

The computer store movement is a symptom of an expanding dollar-volume market. Calculators, minicomputers, and the computer industry in general is in need of new expansion. The days of the big-circus military contracts have passed, and the space program is dwindling. The computer tycoons have saturated banks, insurance companies, and large corporations with Monolith Computers. Now it is time for the small fellows to get into the act.

The computer store in your neighborhood is simply a response to an expanding dollar-volume market that is now being concentrated in common computer-age applications. The most obvious uses of common computers are in homes, small businesses, and as toys. Before attempting to understand the products now available in computer stores, we need a better grasp of terminology and various technical matters.

Computer Jargon Can Mess Your Mind

The best way to pick up the jargon you will need to use in visiting a computer store is to take a hypothetical walk through such a store. Suppose we go along with Tom Swift, Dr. Goode, and their friends to visit a neighborhood computer outlet. Remember, these people are looking for a solution to very real problems. We will see what hurdles they must overcome along the way.

Dr. Goode and his son J. E. find the computer store in a shopping center next to a pet shop. The store is full of people milling around. One group is gathered around a small machine that is playing tic-tac-toe with a customer. Another group is standing in front of a rack of books, intently reading. A salesman is explaining a technical fact to two teenagers at the counter.

The saleswoman who greets Dr. Goode and J. E. immediately determines that the two of them are novices. She has just talked to Tom Swift and realized that he as well as the Goodes need to be informed of basics.

"Dr. Goode, I'd like you and J. E. to meet Tom Swift from Tom's Motorcycle Shop. Tom's thinking of buying a personal computer to help out with some of his inventory problems. I've invited him to our weekly lecture on Thursday evening. Perhaps you'd like to come too."

"Is the lecture oriented to beginners or do we have to prepare beforehand?" asked Dr. Goode, after he had acknowledged Tom.

"I'd recommend that you read this book, but of course we'll begin at the beginning at Thursday's lecture," replied the saleswoman as she handed Tom and John a copy of *How to Profit from Your Personal Computer.*

"Oh, thank you," said John. "I hope this is readable. You know J. E. can probably understand computer talk better than I can. I'll buy this for him and let him explain it to me."

The saleswoman laughed and invited them to look around. Then she moved on to speak to another visitor.

Dr. Goode, J. E., and Tom spent several hours in the store. They learned a lot of new words, and somehow the computer jargon began to make sense. They learned that a computer uses *binary* instead of *decimal* arithmetic. Often it is easier to group binary numbers into bit patterns and encode them as *octal* digits instead. For example, the eight-bit pattern

$$01\ 101\ 111$$

is coded into a three octal (1 5 7) pattern, using the BCD table of Fig. 1.4. Only the first eight decimal digits are used in the octal system, and the most significant bits are stripped from the BCD patterns.

In binary subtraction only ones and zeros are allowed. This means that when borrowing from the more significant bit, a *two* is borrowed instead of a one (two is written in binary as 10). For example, 101 minus 11, which equals 10, requires that a *decimal two* be borrowed from the leftmost bit of 101. In short, we must borrow twos instead of tens in binary subtraction.

Tom and Dr. Goode also learned that computers perform two kinds of binary arithmetic: two's complement integer arithmetic and floating-point arithmetic. In two's complement integer calculations, the numbers cannot have decimal points or fractions, and every negative number is the complement of its positive magnitude. For example, adding together the binary numbers of Fig. 3.1(A), we use two's complement integer arithmetic, but for adding together the numbers of Fig. 3.1(B), we use floating-point arithmetic. Tom and Dr. Goode are told to be careful about buying a computer without floating-point arithmetic, because they will need the latter to do dollars and cents calculations for their businesses.

The terms "two's complement" and "ten's complement" come from the way the complement number is calculated. In binary complement calculation, we use $2^4 = 16$, and in decimal complement calculation, we use $10^2 = 100$. Notice that $2^4 = 10000$ in binary and that when using complements, no subtraction (only addition) is performed.

In Fig. 3.1(A), the binary patterns are added together by first converting minus (0110) to its two's complement. In this case, the two's complement of (0110) is (1010) because (10000) − (0110) = (1010) in binary. This is analogous with the ten's complement calculation shown in Fig. 3.1(A) also. In both cases, the carry-out digit is discarded.

Tom Swift and Dr. Goode also learn that personal computers have *instruction sets.* In fact, they discover that various companies sell various kinds of computers, each with its own instruction set, working registers, and unique hardware features. The combination of instructions, registers, and hardware features taken into consideration as a whole comprise the *system architecture.* The system architectures for two different personal computers are shown conceptually in Fig. 3.2.

Figure 3.2 illustrates the circuitry for performing computations in each of the two computers. The arithmetic logic unit (ALU), for example, is a section of the computer whose circuits perform addition,

(A) Two's Complement Integer Addition

Binary

```
   1101
 -(0110)
   ‾‾‾‾
   0111
```

Method: Convert (0110) to (1010) and then add:

```
         1101
        +1010
         ‾‾‾‾
 Carry   0111
```

Decimal Equivalent

```
    13
  -  6
    ‾‾
     7
```

Method: Convert (6) to (100 − 6) = (94) and then add:

```
         13
        +94
         ‾‾
 Carry   07
```

(B) Floating-Point Arithmetic

Binary	*Decimal Equivalent*
101.10	5.50
+ 11.01	+3.25
1000.11	8.75

Method: Add bit-by-bit and carry the zero or one to the next column.

Fig. 3.1 Arithmetic for personal computing

comparisons, and movement of data from the register or main memory of the system. Other parts of the computer temporarily hold binary numbers. The *program counter*, for example, contains the address of the next instruction to be performed by the ALU. The *stack pointer* register holds the address of a number stored in main memory. Usually, the stack register is used to control the order in which programs are run.

The 8080 architecture consists of three pairs of eight-bit working registers. These registers hold operands while they are being processed by the ALU. In addition, the accumulator register A receives data

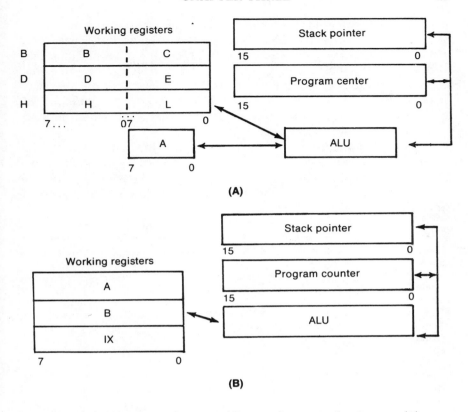

Fig. 3.2 Two different system architectures for personal computers: (A) The 8080 architecture, and (B) the 6800 architecture

from the ALU. The ALU can add the contents of register D, say, to the contents of A and then move the result in A to register B.

The architectures of both machines use a stack pointer register to access a first-in-last-out region of main memory. In addition, the 8080 uses the H-L pair of registers as a means to locate data in main memory. This is done by placing the address of a "mail box" of main memory in the H-L pair before performing an ALU function.

In the 6800 architecture, main memory data is accessed by the IX register, which is added to part of the instruction to come up with the location of data.

The machine architectures of Fig. 3.2 also must be able to fetch machine instructions stored in the main memory. That is, the processors must be able to locate a program before it can be controlled. This job is done by the *program counter register*, which always contains the address of the next program instruction to be executed.

In the short time Tom and the Goodes spent in the computer store, they discovered that computers execute one machine instruction after another unless interrupted by input/output devices. Hence, in addition to normal processing capability, the architecture of a personal computer includes an *interrupt structure*. The importance of the interrupt structure was not clear to them, however, and as it happened, Tom did not come to understand interrupts until years later when he used a computer that was timeshared.

They heard the words "microprogramming" and "read-only-memory," too. Microprogramming is the process of writing firmware programs that are stored in the read-only-memory (ROM). "Software" was a vague term to Tom and John until a fellow shopper showed them the chart of Fig. 3.3.

Octal location	Binary machine instruction			Symbolic assembly instruction	High-level language instruction
0300	00	111	010	LDA B	
0301	00	000	000		
0302	00	000	100	LHLD C	
0303	00	101	010		
0304	00	000	001	ADD M	
0305	00	000	100		
0306	10	000	110	STA X	
0307	00	110	010		LET X = B + C
0310	00	000	010		
0312	00	000	100	HLT	
0400	00	000	011	B: DEFS 3	
0401	00	000	101	C: DEFS 5	
0402	00	000	000	X: DEFS 0	
•		•		•	
•		•		•	
•		•		•	

Fig. 3.3 Levels of software in a personal computer

In Fig. 3.3, the lowest level of programming consists of the binary words of machine language programming. At the next higher level, the symbolic notation of assembly language can be used. In the high-level language instruction, the values of B and C are added together and stored in X.

The 8080 architecture requires loading the H-L registers with the address of B, then of C, and finally of X. These addresses are used to copy the values of B and C into the ALU, where they are added. The result is saved in register A and then copied to the location of X.

Figure 3.3 also demonstrates how a personal computer is programmed at several different levels. At the binary level, the pattern of bits is simply copied into main memory and executed directly by the processor. At the assembly language level, it is necessary to translate the symbols into binary words before executing the program. This job is usually done by another program called the *assembler*. An assembler is a system software module provided by the manufacturer as an aid to programming.

If a program is written in a high-level language like BASIC, then the statement LET X = B + C must be either translated into machine language by a program called a *compiler* or else directly processed by a program called an *interpreter*.

An interpreter differs from a compiler in that it is a program that directly executes the high-level language and bypasses the intermediate steps needed to reduce X = B + C to binary patterns. The interpreter produces slower running programs, but the programs are written and developed quickly. We will use an interpretive version of BASIC for the programs in this book.

Tom and Dr. John learned a few more buzz words before leaving the store. A *loader* is a program that loads other programs into main memory so that they may be run. An *editor* is a program used to prepare other programs for execution. A *utility program* is a system program that is so useful that is it put into a library for anyone to use. Finally, an *operating system* is a program that helps the user deal with the computer at a higher level. In particular, the diskette operating system (DOS) assists users and programmers in using the hardware of most personal computers.

Usually, the DOS is a collection of routines or *subprograms* that perform specific tasks. For example, they drive the input/output devices, manage the memory so that programs can be moved around to make more room for other programs, and assist programming in high-level languages like BASIC. Indeed, since every action permitted in the computer system must be accommodated by the operating system, Tom and Dr. Goode learned that the limitations of the operating system also limit the entire system.

Where We Learn the Limitations of Computers

Tom Swift and Dr. Goode went away from the computer store that day with a feeling of amazement about what computers can do. In order to be fair to the two of them, however, the computer store people should have discussed some of the limitations of computers as well.

Personal computers are limited in two ways, both by their hardware and their software. Recall that hardware is merely an ignorant slave that *may* be able to do what is desired of it but only if proper control is applied. Software, on the other hand, is control; without software, hardware is useless. Let's look first at hardware limitations.

Hardware limits personal computing in three fundamental ways:
1. Speed
2. Capacity
3. I/O

Speed is a limitation that becomes most obvious in scientific applications, but often it enters into routine business applications as well. For example, a local bank may require additional computer power because it must alphabetize its depositors' names before updating their balances. Since it is the internal processing speed of the computer that determines how fast a computer can sort the names into order, we say that the system is *compute-bound*.

The processor of a personal computer may be compute-bound and unable to keep up with the work load expected of it. Thus, the first limitation of a computer is the processor speed itself. This speed is measured in the millions of instructions per second, or MIPS. A typical personal computer is capable of one-tenth to ten MIPS.

The speed of auxiliary storage, whether disk or tape, may also slow a computer down. The line printer or operator may contribute to a slowdown, too. What measures of speed do we apply to these hardware components?

Magnetic tape is used to store programs and data while they are waiting to be processed by the central processor. Disk or diskette (floppy or flexible disks) devices are used in a similar manner but have a lower storage capacity than magnetic tape (see Fig. 3.4).

Tape devices are very slow because they are read from one end to the other whenever data are needed. What is called their *access time* is governed by the speed of the tape drive.

A diskette device is moderately fast because it may be read once for every revolution of the diskette. Typically, the average access time of a diskette is 300 ms (1 ms = 1 millisecond = 1/1000 second). Hence, the diskette can be read over three times a second.

A character printer is relatively slow. In fact, it is usually the bottleneck of the personal computer. Printer speeds are measured in cps (characters per second) or lpm (lines per minute). A 240-cps printer will print less than three 80-character lines per second because of the mechanical delay in returning the print mechanism to the left of the carriage.

A *bidirectional* character printer is a printer that types left-to-right and right-to-left as well. Bidirectional printers are much faster than

Fig. 3.4 A floppy or diskette storage device (*Courtesy*, Madeline Rubin)

ordinary printers because there is no delay in going from one line to the next. An 80-cps bidirectional printer is well suited to most personal computer systems.

When every part of a personal computer is considered, the actual amount of work that can be accomplished may be more than any one of the components appears to be capable of doing. In many cases, however, the actual work performed turns out to be less than it should be according to the independent speeds of the components. What is really desired is high *throughput.* Throughput is a measure of the number of jobs a computer can process. The problem with measuring throughput is that it depends upon the *job mix* .

Job mix is the character of data processing tasks submitted to a computer. The mix determines how much of the time a printer will be used, what percentage of the processor time is to be used, and how frequently the diskette or tape is to be referenced. Only when the job mix is known can the power of a computer system be measured.

A *bench mark program* is a program written to measure the throughput of a system. An example is a program that reads 10,000 names from a diskette, sorts them into alphabetical order, and then prints them on the line printer. This benchmark measures the throughput of diskette, processor, and printer-bound processing. The result of the benchmark will tell us how effective each hardware module is in performing its task under severe conditions.

The second limitation on hardware is the capacity limitation. The most severe capacity restraint is the size of main memory. If a personal computer has 16K of main memory and yet a 20K program is run, or an attempt made to run it, what can be done? The simplest solution may be to purchase more main memory.

When programs and data are not being processed, they are stored on peripheral memory devices, collectively called *auxiliary storage*. A diskette has from 256K to 500K bytes of auxiliary storage capacity. A cassette tape may have 8 MB (megabytes) or more of storage, depending upon its length. Clearly, choosing between tape and diskette involves a trade-off between speed and capacity.

A *cartridge disk* may have the capacity to store from 2.5 MB to 20 MB of programs and data. Such a large capacity disk system offers both speed and capacity, but at high cost to the owner of a personal computer.

A *CCD* (charge-coupled device) *memory* is a semiconductor device quite similar to MOS technology. These memories operate on the basis of moving charges within a semiconducting metal. CCD auxiliary storage is used when seeking a compromise between an expensive disk and a lower speed diskette.

A *bubble memory* is another semiconductor device that stores data as very small moving magnetic spots within a semiconducting lattice. It offers another compromise between disk and diskette.

The greatest limitation for personal computing stems from the fact that I/O devices are mechanical rather than electrical. A printer must actually strike a form in order to make an imprint on the five-part paper. An operator must strike a moving key to enter the data.

Other options for inputting data and programs include *graphics* (a light-pen device and a CRT), *voice response* (computer-generated voice and computer-analyzed sound), and *transducer* (energy conversion from pressure, light, or sound to electrical signals). At the present, unfortunately, these are either too expensive or unreliable to be of use with personal computers. For now, we are limited to slow, noisy, cumbersome mechanical I/O devices.

In short, personal computers must be selected for their measured shortcomings and not their assumed strengths. The only way to determine their actual abilities is to "kick the tires and test drive" them.

How to Kick the Tires

Tom Swift and Dr. Goode finally decided to buy their first personal computer. Several weeks later they returned to the computer shop to evaluate the various kinds available. Let us see how they went about their selection.

Tom Swift's Motorcycle Shop wanted its computer to "remember" a vast number of parts numbers and print lengthy reports on a daily basis. Tom needed a system with the following hardware:

1. 16K main memory for programs
2. Large capacity auxiliary memory for the parts list
3. Rapid bidirectional impact type printer for the reports

Questions he had to ask were "What language is the program to be written in?" "How large is a 'large' parts list?," and "How fast is a 'rapid' bidirectional printer?"

Tom and his partner Jeff analyzed their inventory *data base* and discovered to their amazement that they stockpiled an average of 100,000 parts per month. Multiplying the number of digits, letters, and special characters used to record each part number and description by 100,000, they arrived at a storage capacity of 1.5 MB.

Furthermore, Tom and Jeff needed a high-speed "impact" type printer to produce their reports. They chose a bidirectional *dot-matrix printer* (5 by 7 array of dots for each character printed) because it has high speed (80 cps), low cost, and will impact through five carbon copies.

When it came to estimating the size of main memory needed, Tom and Jeff were puzzled. They had not considered their software problem and were unable to estimate the ultimate size of the control program that would have to be programmed before they could use their newly purchased hardware. Exactly how they faced this problem is the subject of Chap. 4.

Dr. John Goode and his son selected a personal computer based upon the following goals:

1. 8K main memory for the programs
2. Moderately large auxiliary memory with rapid look-up capability for updating the accounts of each patient
3. A printer with high-quality printing for making billing statements once each month

Dr. John had been at a loss when it came to choosing the size of main memory. His son emphasized the need for BASIC as the programming language, however, and since the BASIC they selected requires 8K of main memory, they purchased a system with a memory to fit that need.

The clinic billing computer had to be able to update (change) the current balances on all patients that arrive and depart during each day. Thus, it was important to have good *access times* for the data base (records containing the doctors' patient information). A dual diskette system was selected because it offers rapid update for a reasonable cost and because the volume of data is small enough to be stored on a few removable diskettes.

Finally, Dr. Goode selected a 30-cps printer because it typed like a typewriter and was inexpensive. Selecting a slower printer was a difficult choice for the doctor and his son because they had hoped to be able to print all the monthly statements on the last day of each month. At a speed of 30 cps, they estimated it would take their personal computer two to three days to complete the monthly statements. Dr. Goode felt that the trade-off was worthwhile, however, because he wanted his patients to obtain a statement that was warm and personal. The dot-matrix font of the higher speed printer might offend his patients because they would know that the statements were printed by machine.

Tom Swift and Dr. Goode more or less stumbled into the computer age by way of accident, need, and good fortune. Luckily, they were also intelligent men and made wise decisions about the hardware they bought. Here is a recipe for selecting hardware and software that may be of use to others.

TOTAL SYSTEM COST
  1. *Hardware, plus*
  2. *System software, plus*
  3. *Cost of applications software, plus*
  4. *Cost of adequate service*

STEP 1.   What are your requirements?
   Identify:
   1. The applications programs you will write or buy
   2. The size of main memory that the applications programs plus the operating system will use
   3. The speed and size of peripherals needed to achieve the necessary throughput

STEP 2.   Configure a tentative system.
   Based on Step 1, draw a block diagram of the hardware you anticipate needing and determine whether this system falls within your cost constraints.

STEP 3.   What system software is essential?
   1. Operating system: tape, disk, diskette
   2. Compiler or interpreter: FORTRAN, BASIC
   3. Editor, debug, utility package

STEP 4.   Eliminate competitive systems that fail to meet your requirements.
   1. Do not buy "promised hardware." Consider only those systems that meet your needs today.

2. Check all features of the software. Does BASIC have file commands? Strings?
3. Can you get serviced easily? What happens when the system breaks down?

STEP 5. *What can you do without?*

When confronted by a cost crunch, what parts of the system can be sacrificed? Often this question reduces to a hardware versus software cost trade-off. Bare hardware is cheaper than programmed hardware. Can you afford to do the initial program development yourself?

STEP 6. *Benchmark.*

Write short test programs to exercise the candidates for purchase. Measure the throughput, and emphasize types of computing:
1. Compute-bound test: Calculate A + B thousands of times, for example.
2. I/O-bound test: Access diskettes and use printer thousands of times, for example.
3. Error-bound test: Purposely cause errors to test the system's ability to recover. For example, compute a zero divide: A/0.

STEP 7. *Readjust your initial configuration.*

Re-evaluate the system tentatively designed in Step 2. Does it still meet your needs? Would it be wiser to purchase less main memory and more diskettes? Did you discover that the operating system was too large to run on the system you thought to be adequate? Is the system fast enough?

STEP 8. *Get bids.*

Visit all the computer stores in your area and have them give you estimates on the system you reconfigured in Step 7.

STEP 9. *Don't forget programming costs.*

This step brings us to the next topic of discussion.

Hardware Is Only Half the Solution

The other half of the solution is the part that controls the hardware: software. Unfortunately, while the LSI revolution has diminished the cost of hardware to near the vanishing point, the high cost of programming is getting still higher.

In the next chapter we will analyze the problem of programming, give recommendations on how to minimize costs, and provide a basis for the orderly production of high-level language programs.

Chapter Four

WHY CAN'T A COMPUTER BE MORE LIKE A MAN?

The first time we tried it, the rocket made a hissing sound, turned on its side, and churned dust for twenty feet behind its launch pad. We all took cover, of course, and when it was through moving, the neighborhood kids stood wide-eyed and with their mouths open as dad and I approached the wounded beast. Dad picked it up and began making repairs. I remember today how he set about starting over: "At least the motor works. Next time we should get 'bout 50 yards of altitude out of it."

Hermes Nub, 1968

Hardware Is Easy but Software Is Hard

The LSI revolution made it possible to build computer hardware so inexpensively that now software costs dominate the overall system cost. One reason for the astounding success in hardware is that it is well understood by its builders. Computer software, on the other hand, is poorly understood. As a result, software is costly, and many people decide to become programmers in order to save the money that would otherwise be needed to purchase programs. But before embarking on a large programming project, it is necessary to gain an appreciation for programming. In short, we must come to understand software.

Actually, the amount of expertise needed to write computer programs is not as great as it may appear at first. In fact, nearly anyone can learn to program. To become a good programmer, however, may require exceptional aptitude or hours of practice. Before you decide whether you are capable of becoming a good programmer, learn the fundamental lessons known to expert programmers, and don't fall for the Blinking Light Myth.

The Blinking Light Myth

Computers, with their massive arrays of blinking lights and

myriads of components, are complicated machines built by geniuses who are the only people able to understand them.

versus

Computer hardware, blinking lights and all, is the simplest part of a computer system and well understood by thousands of people who are not geniuses.

The Blinking Light Myth must no longer prevent ordinary people from using personal computers. There is a factor that should be considered by any user of personal computers, however, and this is the Software Myth.

The Software Myth

The software needed to make a computer system function properly and do the job that it is supposed to do can be considered a minor obstacle to the total system functioning.

versus

Software (the programs that control computer hardware) is the most costly component of a personal computer system, and yet it is the least understood component of a total computer system.

Unfortunately, the Software Myth has trapped many naive users of computers. Software must be designed, implemented, maintained, documented, and, most importantly, updated periodically. It can break down and lead to disaster more easily than hardware can because it is more complicated than most hardware. What can be done to avoid or reduce the impact of the Software Myth?

Programming

Programming is the art and engineering skill used to implement the control portion of a computer. Programs are developed by specifying detailed steps (called instructions) for each action to be performed by the hardware.

What is it about programming that requires skill? How can we minimize the effort needed to write successful programs for personal computers? To answer these questions, we must study three major aspects of programming that have been discovered by programmers during the last few decades.

1. Abstraction
2. Interpretation
3. The BJ Result

A good understanding of these three aspects in relation to the Software Factor can lead to a reduction in the cost of programming.

Abstraction is the process of removing details from a programming task so that it can be understood. In most programming tasks, *levels of abstraction,* rather than a single abstraction, unfold as the program is developed. As an illustration, consider the following problem.

Jack wishes to write a program for his personal computer that will compute the average of some numbers. He could use this program to average test scores, for example, or to compute the average height of professional basketball players. If he is clever enough, he can write the program so that it is general enough to work for two, ten, or a hundred numbers. Jack's first level of abstraction is in Fig. 4.1.

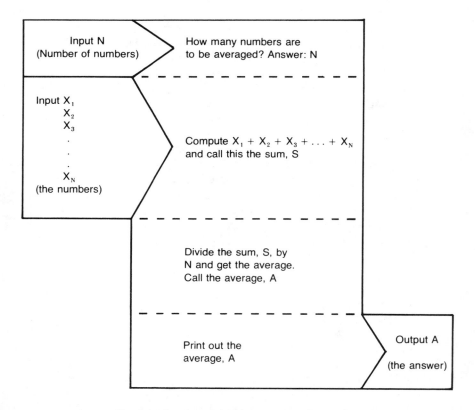

Fig. 4.1   An abstraction for an averaging program

The abstracted program of Fig. 4.1 can be readily understood by anyone who reads it. The purpose of such an abstraction is to assist Jack in writing a correct program while simultaneously providing a document for himself and others to read. Once this document becomes

1. PROGRAM: This Program Computes the Average of N Numbers

2. DATA:
    N = number of numbers to be averaged, initially input
    X_i i-th number read into computer, initially input
    S = sum of X_i for i = 1 to N, initially zero
    A = average, that is, the answer, initially unknown

3. INSTRUCTION STEPS;
    3.1 Input N
    3.2 Set S = 0, initially, but . . .
    3.3 Add up each X_i as it is input; this is S, step by step
    3:4 Once final S is computed, compute A = S/N
    3.5 Output A
    3.6 Stop

Fig. 4.2 Another level of abstraction for an averaging program

```
10 REM   COMPUTE THE AVERAGE OF N NUMBERS.
20 PRINT "HOW MANY NUMBERS?"
30 INPUT N
40 LET S=0
50 FOR I=1 TO N
52 PRINT "GIVE ME A NUMBER"
54 INPUT X
56 LET S=S+X
58 NEXT I
60 LET A=S/N
70 PRINT "THE AVG. IS ...",A
80 END
```

Fig. 4.3 BASIC language abstraction of Fig. 4.2

available, Jack or anyone else trying to understand the averaging program can attempt the next level of abstraction, as shown in Fig. 4.2.

    Figure 4.2 gives the program in more detail, and yet the program is still too vague to be understood by a computer. The abstraction of Fig. 4.2 must be reduced even further before it can be input to a computer. A final form of the abstraction is shown in Fig. 4.3.

    We shall call the languages used to specify abstractions such as those shown in Figs. 4.1, 4.2, and 4.3 *blueprint languages.* A variety of blueprint specification languages are in use by professional programmers. The blueprint languages used in this book are the following:

        $BLUE_0$: Process chart of Fig. 4.1
        $BLUE_1$: Pseudo code of Fig. 4.2
        $BLUE_2$: BASIC program of Fig. 4.3

The manner in which we begin with $BLUE_0$ and add greater levels of detail is called *top-down refinement*. The particular languages used to write programs by the top-down refinement method is not important. The fact that top-down refinement is used, however, is of considerable importance. Top-down refinement reduces errors in programming and leads to reliable, low-cost, and well documented programs.

In Fig. 4.3 we have specified what we want the computer to do in a $BLUE_2$ language that can be understood by a personal computer. But first the personal computer system must be equipped with software to translate the BASIC language. For the moment, we assume that the BASIC software is provided. What does the computer do?

In step 10 we have used a REM statement to *rem*ark that this is an averaging program. The remark has no effect on the computer and is merely an aid to human understanding.

In step 20 the computer is told to display "HOW MANY NUMBERS?" on the display terminal and then wait for the operator to type in a number. This number, N, is stored in step 3.

In step 40 the sum S is set to zero. Steps 50 to 58 are repeated N times, once for each value of I = 1, 2, 3, ... N. This process, called a program loop, is a very useful programming technique.

In BASIC, all data are assigned a symbolic storage location in the main memory by using the LET statement. The FOR statement is used along with the NEXT statement to cause looping. The INPUT and PRINT statements have obvious meanings, and END brings the program to a stop.

Steps 50 to 58 loop over and over again until I = (N + 1). In step 56, the partial sum of all of the X_i's is accumulated in location S. For example, if $X_1 = 5$, $X_2 = 100$, and $X_3 = 1000$, then the loop for I = 1, 2, and 3 would produce values of S as follows:

I	*S*
1	5
2	105
3	1105

The levels of abstraction illustrated by Figs. 4.1, 4.2, and 4.3 are said to reduce errors and thereby reduce programming costs. Intuitively, we can see why this may be true. Each level is a guide in thinking about the problem. The blueprints assist our understanding, and as a result, the programs are clearer and less prone to errors than they might have been. Even so, it is possible to overlook something, and errors may creep in. Such errors, committed accidentally during program development, are called *bugs*. How can we prevent bugs in programs?

A wise programmer combats bugs by *probing* each section of a program. In Fig. 4.4 we have rewritten the programs of Figs. 4.2 and

(A) BLUE₁ Abstraction

1. PROGRAM: This Probed Program Computes an Average of N Numbers

2. DATA:
    N = number of numbers, initially input
    X_i = numbers to be averaged, initially input
    S = sum of X_i's, initially zero
    A = average, initially unknown
    P = probe count, initially zero

3. INSTRUCTION STEPS
    3.1 Input N; Output N
    3.2 Set S = 0 and P = 1
    3.3 Repeat for I = 1 up to N
        Input X; Output X
        Sum S; Increment P by 1
    3.4 Compute A = S/N
    3.5 Output A an P
    3.6 Stop

(B) BLUE₂ Abstraction (BASIC)

```
10 REM   COMPUTE THE AVERAGE OF N NUMBERS.
11 REM OUTPUT PROBES : N, X, ...X, A, P
20 PRINT "HOW MANY NUMBERS?"
30 INPUT N
31 PRINT N
40 LET S=0
41 LET P=1
50 FOR I=1 TO N
52 PRINT "GIVE ME A NUMBER"
54 INPUT X
55 PRINT X
56 LET S=S+X
57 LET P=P+1
58 NEXT I
60 LET A=S/N
70 PRINT "AVERAGE IS...", A, "  PROBE IS...", P
80 END
```

Fig. 4.4 Probed programs for averaging

4.3 to include prevention measures that will help detect any bugs that may exist. The newly revised BLUE₂ program of Fig. 4.4(B) causes the computer to output the input data so that the user can verify whether it has been input correctly. Also, the number of times through the loop (statements 50–58) is computed by P to give another indication of correctness. Even so, the program of Fig. 4.4(B) may not function correctly if additional checks are not made. Can you spot a weakness in this version of the averaging program?

To be safe, a wise programmer would add the following code to the program of Fig. 4.4(B):

```
32   IF N > 0 THEN 40
34   PRINT "N MUST BE POSITIVE"
36   GOTO 30
```

This segment of code causes the program to be repeated from statement 30 onward if the value input to *N* is less than or equal to zero. In BASIC, such decisions are made by an IF-THEN or IF-GOTO statement. When the value of an IF-GOTO statement is TRUE, the next statement to be executed is given by the GOTO portion (THEN portion) of the statement. When the IF-GOTO statement is FALSE, the next statement executed is the one immediately following the IF-GOTO statement.

In step 36, the BASIC statement says GOTO 30. This is an unconditional branch that forces the computer to execute statement 30 immediately following the GOTO 30 statement at step 36.

Abstraction is a very useful tool in programming. It is used to hide detailed information from view until needed by the programmer. When sufficient understanding is gained at a higher level of abstraction, the next lower level is constructed by adding more detail. This process of top-down refinement is repeated until a level is reached that a computer can understand.

Exactly how a computer is able to understand a level of abstraction like BASIC is a matter of "interpretation" versus "compilation." To understand these two important concepts of computing we need to learn some more computer slang.

Learning Some More Computer Slang

The second most important lesson for programmers is the fact that the computer itself can be the biggest obstacle or the greatest help in writing a program. Careful selection of a $BLUE_2$ (high-level) language and other software aids can help relieve you of tiresome hours at a hot terminal.

A *text editor* is a program that helps a programmer input, modify, and copy programs into memory. An editor is used, for example, to insert corrected segments of program into an existing incorrect program. An editor can be used to search for a word or words within a program and replace them with other words.

The editor works on a program by treating it as a collection of *strings*. A string is a run of characters like the letters on this page. Strings usually have no value other than that of the characters contained within the string.

Replacing a string with another string is an operation performed by most text editors. Inserting and deleting statements of a program are string operations when performed by an editor.

An *interpreter* is a program that executes other programs. A BASIC interpreter, for example, is capable of reading the BASIC programs of Figs. 4.3 and 4.4 and performing the steps indicated by the programs. The most important feature of an interpreter is the fact that it *directly* operates upon the $BLUE_2$ specification language without additional levels of abstraction being applied. Thus an interpreter is a program that can perform the steps indicated by a blueprint in exactly the same way a man would perform the steps. An interpreter is capable of doing what we have instructed it to do without further processing or additional top-down refinement. Compare an interpreter, for example, with a compiler that produces an additional level of blueprint.

A *compiler* is a program that performs an additional top-down refinement. The input to a compiler is a program (for example, BASIC statements) written in a BLUE specification language. The output of a compiler is another blueprint language specification of the problem. Typically, the output of a compiler is a machine language specification.

Compilers read *source* statements into main memory and produce *object code* statements. For example, if the source statements were in BASIC blueprint form, then the object code output would be a machine language blueprint for some machine. Thus we could envision the following top-down refinements:

$BLUE_0$: Process language
$BLUE_1$: Pseudo code
$BLUE_2$: BASIC language
$BLUE_3$: Machine language

A compiler replaces human effort by translating a program from $BLUE_2$ form to $BLUE_3$ form. Therefore, a compiler is a useful aid in preparing a program.

Figure 4.5 summarizes the program preparation cycle for both interpreter and compiler languages. There are advantages and disadvantages to each approach. Interpreters execute code much more slowly than is possible with a compiled machine language. Compilers retard program development because translation into another level of abstraction must be done once before the program can be run.

Three rules-of-thumb may be cautiously applied when deciding between interpreters, machine language, and compilers. These rules have been observed to be true in most, if not all, cases.

Rule of Speed: Programming speed is independent of the language being used; the rate of statement production depends upon the application and not the language.

This rule says that the productivity of a programmer is fixed by the application at so many statements per day. The language, however,

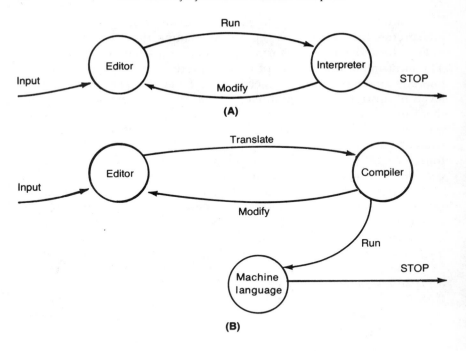

Fig. 4.5 Comparison of interpreters and compilers: (A) Interpretive programming, and (B) compilation programming

may be a low-level language or a high-level language. That is, it may be a BLUE$_1$ or a BLUE$_3$ language. This rule leads to a corrollary.

Rule of Power: The power of a high-level language is inversely proportional to the number of statements needed to solve an application problem.

This rule clearly demands that we employ the highest level language possible in developing applications programs. We can maximize the speed at which a program is written by choosing a high-level language that requires the fewest program steps to get the job done.

Once a high-level language is chosen, should it be an interpreter or a compiler that executes the program? The following rule reveals that an interpreter saves a programmer much more of his or her time than a compiler.

Rule of Convenience: An interpreter executes code slower than compiled code can be executed, but interpretation accelerates program development by a factor of 10 to 100 times.

The interpretive program may also run from 10 to 100 times slower than the code produced by a compiler. Whether running speed is important or not is a question answered only when the problem is tested. In most cases, the programs suggested in this book will run faster than the human or mechanical input or output device can appreciate.

Interpretation of $BLUE_2$ specifications combined with top-down refinement as a programming tool will lead to successful programming. To gain full appreciation for this approach we will study numerous examples in detail. But first, we must study the building blocks of programming as supplied by the Boehm and Jacopini result.

The Art of Programming in Spite of BASIC

While BASIC lacks many of the features desirable in a programming language, it does have three distinct advantages:
1. BASIC is "high-level"
2. BASIC is interpretive
3. BASIC is available

The first two of these advantages have been discussed briefly in the previous section. The third feature is important because LSI hardware is useless at any price without software aids. The BASIC interpreter is available on a variety of computers at relatively low cost.

BASIC is widely available because it is simple. Simple languages are quickly implemented on low-cost personal computers because the effort needed to implement the interpreter or compiler is minimal.

Unfortunately, the notion of a single BASIC interpreter for all machines is a myth. There are as many versions of BASIC as there are personal computers. Beware of the differences, and do not fall for the Standard BASIC Myth, which may be expressed by the first of the following two propositions.

There is a language called BASIC, or Dartmouth BASIC, that is interpretive and will allow any BASIC program to be run on any personal computer with a BASIC interpreter.
versus
There are many dialects of BASIC, each one slightly different from the other, and thus few BASIC programs will run on any personal computer without modification.

The versions of BASIC, in fact, are legion. Tiny BASIC, or TBX, is a version that barely resembles the original Dartmouth BASIC. A

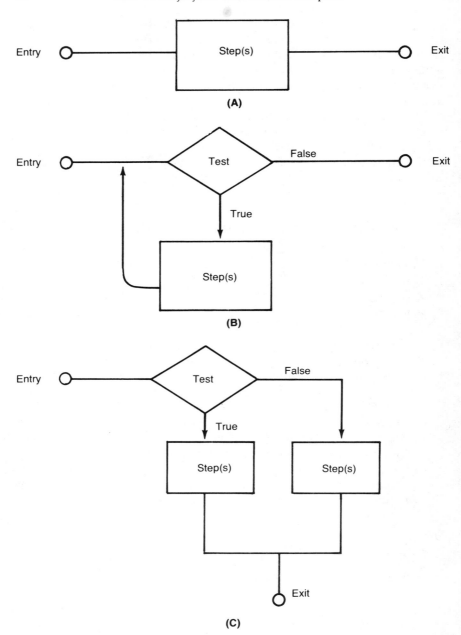

Fig. 4.6 The three building blocks of Boehm and Jacopini: (A) Sequence, (B) Repeat, and (C) Choice

5K BASIC and an 8K BASIC are other forms available to support various features of the full language.

The version of BASIC used in this book is BASIC-PLUS. Its most important functions are listed below:

1. Floating-point arithmetic
2. Array structures
3. File structures
4. Strings
5. Built-in functions

The capabilities that these functions give to a personal computer are listed below in corresponding order:

1. Dollars and cents calculations are possible.
2. Programming is simplified.
3. Storage for large amounts of data is provided.
4. Human input and output formatting ability is provided.
5. Programming effort is reduced.

Careful selection of a BASIC interpreter can save hours in program development. Likewise, careful coordination of BASIC, an editor, and the hardware can prevent unexpected problems that may turn out to be very costly.

Once the language has been selected and studied to reveal its capability, we must learn to use it in formulating blueprints. To do this with the greatest amount of success, we must understand the Boehm-Jacopini result.

The Boehm-Jacopini Result

Every program can be written using combinations of only three control constructs. The proper application of the three fundamental constructs of Fig. 4.6 is sufficient to write all computer programs.

This startling fact has profound implications for the programs that we will write. We can use these building blocks in a variety of ways and in numerous combinations. Within sections of a program we may apply these constructs over and over again, with no other construct being needed.

The three constructs of Fig. 4.6 hold great promise for simplifying programming. Exactly how can they be applied? The corresponding BASIC statements we will use in each case are shown in Fig. 4.7. Notice in both figures that each structure has a single entry and single exit. The flow of control enters each structure in only one place and exits

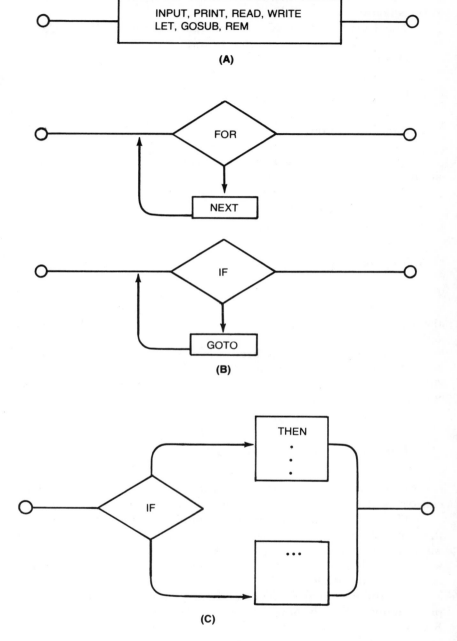

Fig. 4.7 BASIC building blocks in accordance with the Boehm-Jacopini Result: (A) Sequence, (B) Repeat, and (C) Choice

in only one place. Thus these are the simplest structures possible that provide enough "power" to write *any* program.

Figure 4.8(A) is another version of the program in Fig. 4.4(B). We say a BASIC program is *structured* if it is written as a collection of the three essential blocks in the form shown in Fig. 4.8(B). Each structured program in this book can be written in other ways just as Fig. 4.4(B) has been, but it is the author's intention to persuade you to adopt a discipline of programming that will be of great value when you are faced with much larger programming tasks.

In summary, the art of programming in spite of BASIC is carefully to select a dialect of BASIC that serves an intended purpose and to use structuring techniques and the top-down refinement process discussed earlier. In addition, you should use common sense, not fall for the Blinking Light Myth, and be aware of the Software Factor.

Custom Software Versus Store Bought

There are many times when writing programs for your own personal computer is a task of questionable value. Possibly the program can be purchased at a price too low to be resisted. A personal computer may be purchased with an option to buy a set of programs at a reasonable price, for example, or you may simply not have time to develop the programs.

Inevitably, every owner of a personal computer will have to decide between developing a program or collection of programs (called a *package*) and buying the package that matches their needs. For this reason, we need to learn how custom software compares to the store-bought kind.

```
10 REM STRUCTURED VERSION OF AVERAGE PROGRAM
12 REM F IS A FLAG FOR STRUCTURING PURPOSES
14 LET S=0
15 LET F=0
16 LET P=1
17 IF F=1 THEN 30
19 PRINT "INPUT N"
20 INPUT N
22 PRINT N
25 IF N>0 THEN 28
26 LET F=0
28 LET F=1
29 GOTO 17
30 FOR I=1 TO N
32 INPUT X
34 PRINT X
36 LET S=S+X
38 LET P=P+1
40 NEXT I
50 LET A=S/N
60 PRINT A, P
70 END
```

(A)

Fig. 4.8 Structured version of the revised program of Fig. 4.4 (B)

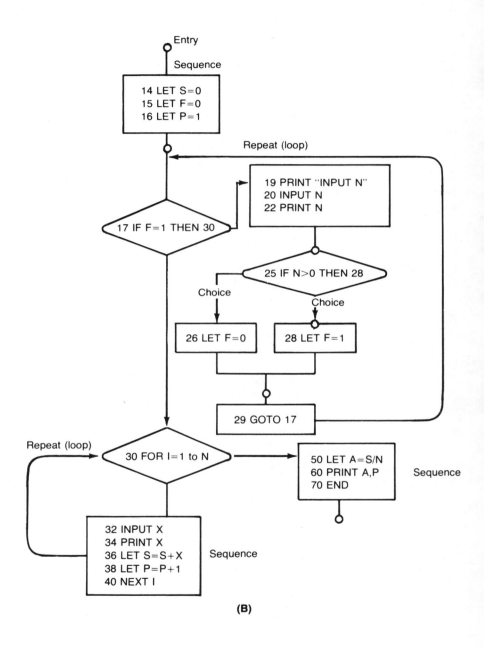

Fig. 4.8 Continued

A custom software package is a collection of programs written for a specific application. The programming is done by a hired programmer or by the owner of the personal computer himself.

A store-bought package is a collection of programs developed for a general area of applications. The idea behind "turnkey" packages is that they are general enough to work for many, many people.

What Is a Store-Bought Package?

What do you get when buying a package? A software package is a vague item because there is no legal definition for a program. In some cases, programs have been treated the same as inventions, whereas in other cases the "inventor" of a program has been denied the right to patent his program.

In some cases, programs have been defined as a creative work that may be protected under a copyright. Such programs may thus be compared to a book, record, or sheet music. The buyer is free to use it, but he cannot produce copies for sale.

In most cases, programs are defined as trade secrets and are protected like any other trade secrets. The "secret" is let out only to those willing to sign a nondisclosure contract and pay a fee for the use of the program.

The notion of a computer program as a legal entity must be settled before we know exactly what it means to buy a package. Typically, purchase of a package is a license to run someone else's program on your personal computer. As such, there are three major questions to be answered when purchasing a package:

1. What is the form of the package? Am I buying the *source* language program or the *object* language program?

2. What am I entitled to do with the package? Can I duplicate it, resell it, loan it to a friend, or am I given the right to use it only on my personal computer?

3. Who is responsible for the program? If it has a flaw and someone is injured because of the flaw, who is responsible? If the program breaks, who is responsible for repairing it?

A major advantage of purchased packages is that they are immediately available. If a package meets expectations, it can be purchased and used without further delay.

Finally, it should be remembered that such packages are designed for the general user. This often means that a specific user will be forced to conform to procedures that are not comfortable. Is the inconvenience worth it?

What Is Custom Software?

Custom software is tailored to the needs of a specific application. For example, Dr. Goode may be able to purchase a package to process his billing data, but he may need a specially customized package to do special things. For example, Dr. Goode's system may have to print reminders to special patients telling them that they are due for their yearly check-up.

In addition to the questions raised by purchasing a package, the custom package approach also poses questions:

1. How long will it take to produce the package? How much will it cost? How well will it perform?
2. How can I be sure the program will do what I asked for? How reliable is the vendor? What can I do if the project is not completed to my satisfaction?

In short, custom packages take longer but give the buyer more for their money. The custom programming project involves a bigger risk, but the buyer learns more from the end result. Finally, the custom package does the exact job intended, if in fact the programmer understands what it is you want.

RULE TO THE WISE: BEWARE OF THE COMPUTER CHARLATANS

What Trade-Offs Are

In our discussion thus far every alternative has proven to have both strong and weak points. It is the responsibility of the buyer and user to make intelligent choices when selecting hardware, software, and packages. Some trade-offs are listed below as a reminder and summary:

Hardware:
    Tape versus disk
    Fast printer versus "quality" printer
    Small main memory versus large main memory
Software:
    Assembler versus high-level language
    Compiler versus interpreter
    Custom package versus store-bought package
    Contract software versus do-it-yourself software

Of course, many of the choices are preordained by the equipment available and the pressures of time and money. Whatever the choices may be, we must delve deeper into software practices to become more aware of the important features of a well-designed program.

Operator Lead-Through and Other Virtues

Once we have a clear understanding of the trade-offs and problems in personal computing, we can begin the task of developing personalized systems. In general, this means developing programs that perform the functions we envisioned when the computer was purchased. Before we tackle this subject in the following chapters, a final word or two on style is needed.

Menu Programming

The idea behind personal computing is that nearly everyone should be able to benefit from a computer. Actually, it is difficult to make a computer system usable unless the system is humanized by paying careful attention to the human/machine interface. This idea and others will be illustrated by the following example.

Tom Swift and Dr. Goode are good businessmen. Each knows that his personal computer is actually "free" because of the tax advantage he will enjoy over the years of its use. They decide to use their personal computers to calculate the depreciation schedule from their investments. Indeed, they want to calculate three separate schedules to see how to maximize their tax returns. The three methods to be selected are displayed in the following "menu":

SELECT ONE OF THE FOLLOWING:
1.   Straight-Line Depreciation
2.   Sum-of-the-Years-Digits Method
3.   Declining-Balance Method

Enter (1, 2, OR 3)?

ARE YOU SURE (Y OR N)?

The menu program for the depreciation package is shown in Fig. 4.9 and illustrates the virtuous practice of *operator lead-through*. Operator lead-through is a method of guiding system users by prompting and directing them along acceptable paths through the program. Lead-through is essential in interactive systems because it reduces errors and reduces the amount of effort required by a noncomputer person to use a computer.

The program of Fig. 4.9(C) uses several features of BASIC which we have discussed before. In line 250, the PRINT statement is used

(A) BLUE₀

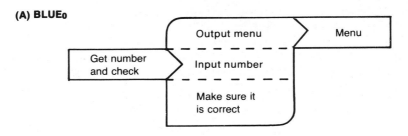

(B) BLUE₁

1. PROGRAM: Menu for Depreciation Methods
2. DATA:
    K = Number selected, initially unknown
    A$ = String ("Y" or "N"), initially unknown
3. STEPS:
    3.1 Display menu
    3.2 Get number K
    3.3 Check to make sure; get A$
    3.4 If not OK, then repeat from step 3.1
    3.5 If OK, then activate proper program
    3.6 Stop

(C) BLUE₂

```
200 REM MENU FOR DEPRECIATION METHODS
210 PRINT "SELECT ONE OF THE FOLLOWING"
220 PRINT "1. STRAIGHT-LINE METHOD."
230 PRINT "2. SUM-OF-THE-YEARS-DIGITS METHOD."
240 PRINT "3. DECLINING-BALANCE METHOD."
250 PRINT
260 PRINT "ENTER (1, 2, OR 3) ?";
270 INPUT K
280 PRINT "ARE YOU SURE(Y OR N) ?";
285 DIM A$[1]
290 INPUT A$
300 IF A$="N" THEN 210
301 REM *************************************
302 REM    GOTO APPROPRIATE PROGRAM
303 REM *************************************
320 IF K=1 THEN 360
330 IF K=2 THEN 380
340 IF K=3 THEN 400
350 GOTO 210
351 REM *************************************
352 REM   SUBPROGRAMS, ONE FOR EACH METHOD
353 REM *************************************
360 GOSUB 450
370 STOP
380 GOSUB 650
390 STOP
400 GOSUB 850
410 STOP
420 END
```

Fig. 4.9 Menu program for the depreciation programs

to generate an empty line in the display so that a space is produced between the menu lines. The semicolons in the question lines 260 and 280 cause inputs at 270 and 290, respectively, to be made on the same line as the question-marked lines.

Line 300 shows how the string variable A$ is used to compare string values "N." (The $ next to any letter is used to name strings in BASIC.) In this way the human operator can enter "Y" or "N" to the question rather than be restricted to numbers.

The program of Fig. 4.9 demonstrates once again the principles of top-down refinement and error checking. Notice that only values of K of 1, 2, or 3 are allowed in lines 320 through 350. The user is forced to give valid input. Also, the user is prompted to check input before the program continues, as shown in line 280.

The next step in the top-down design of the depreciation program is to refine the GOSUB statements at 360, 380, and 400. The GOSUB statement in BASIC has the following effect:

1. Control passes to the line number given in the GOSUB.
2. When a RETURN statement is encountered, control returns to the line following the GOSUB.

Therefore the GOSUB 450 statement at line 360 passes control to line 450. The control returns to line 370 when a RETURN statement is encountered somewhere beyond statement 450. This kind of program control is called *subroutining*.

The subroutine at line 450 must be a program to compute the straight-line depreciation of a tax-deductible purchase. The formula for this calculation is given from the initial cost, COST, minus the final salvage value, SALVAGE VALUE, divided by the equipment's estimated life in years, LIFE, as follows:

$$\text{ANNUAL DEPRECIATION} = \frac{\text{COST} - \text{SALVAGE VALUE}}{\text{LIFE}}$$

For example, if Tom Swift pays $7,000 for his personal computer and he estimates its value at $2,000 at the end of a five-year depreciation period, then the annual depreciation on his personal computer will be:

$$\text{ANNUAL DEPRECIATION} = \frac{7,000 - 2,000}{5}$$
$$= \$1,000 \text{ a year}$$

We can develop the BLUE programs for this method as shown in Fig. 4.10. These programs would be included along with the menu program of Fig. 4.9.

(A) BLUE₀

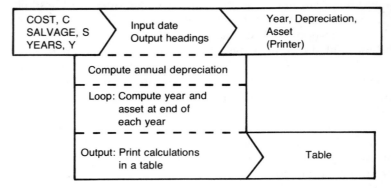

(B) BLUE₁

1. PROGRAM: Subroutine for Straight-Line Method
2. DATA:
    C = cost, initially input
    S = salvage value, initially input
    Y = years, initially input
    A_1 = asset at end of each year, given
    I = loop counter for each year, given
    A_2 = annual depreciation, computed
3. STEPS:
    3.1 Get C, S, and Y
    3.2 Display table headings on printer
    3.3 Compute A_2. Set A_1 = C, initially
    3.4 Repeat the following:
        3.4.1 Print table entries
        3.4.2 Subtract annual depreciation from asset
    3.5 Return to calling program

(C) BLUE₂

```
450 REM   ST. LINE DEPR. ROUTINE.
455 REM   USES C, S, Y, A1, A2, I
460 PRINT "COST=";
470 INPUT C
480 PRINT "SALVAGE=";
490 INPUT S
500 PRINT "LIFE=";
510 INPUT Y
520 REM   DISPLAY TABLE HEADINGS
530 PRINT#4, "YEAR          DEPRECIATION          ASSET"
540 LET A2=(C-S)/Y
550 LET A1=C
560 REM REPEAT LOOP
570 FOR I=1 TO Y
580 LET A1=A1-A2
590 PRINT#4, I, A2, A1
600 NEXT I
610 RETURN
```

Fig. 4.10 Blueprints for the straight-line method

The BASIC program of Fig. 4.10(C) demonstrates once again the value of top-down refinement as a programming method. In addition, we also see how the line printer is used to output the table. In lines 530 and 590, the output is directed to the line printer instead of the terminal as before. This is signified to the BASIC interpreter by including the *logical unit* number, #4.

In addition, the program of Fig. 4.10(C) shows how we continue to use the structuring blocks of the Boehm and Jacopini Result. In lines 450 to 560 we need only sequence control, whereas in lines 570 to 600 we use the loop (repeat) construction.

Sum-of-Digits

The second depreciation routine uses an accelerated depreciation schedule. Dr. Goode feels that computers are subject to rapid aging because of their tendency to become obsolete. In fact, he is already thinking of a bigger and better personal computer that would replace the first one he purchased. Therefore, it may be an advantage to depreciate the system more rapidly in the first few years, and then more slowly toward the end of the five-year life. Thus, in the Sum-of-the-Years-Digits Method, the annual depreciation changes from year to year. In terms of the BASIC program, we compute the depreciation value by the following formula:

$$\text{Depreciation in year T} = 2\,\frac{((Y + 1) - T)(C - S)}{(Y + 1)Y}$$

where Y, C, and S represent the year, initial cost, and salvage value, and T represents the year.

The routine for calculating depreciation using this method is exactly the same as the previous routine except that we delete line 540 and insert line 575:

```
575   LET A2 = 2 * ((Y + 1) − I) * (C − S)/((Y + 1) *Y)
```

Notice that the value of T in this formula is replaced by the year I. The program in its modified form is written in lines 650 to 810. This experience is left for the reader. (Hint: Use your text editor to move a copy to lines 650–810; then replace line 740.).

Declining Balance

The third method of calculating depreciation is used more widely than the Sum-of-Digits method because of its simplicity. It is easier to calculate by hand while retaining the feature of an accelerated depreciation schedule.

The Declining Balance method computes the amount of depreciation for each year by multiplying the asset times a rate, P. For example, if the rate is 25 percent, then we would obtain a 10-year schedule for $10,000 as follows:

Year	Asset	Depreciation
1	10,000	0.25 (10,000) = 2,500
2	7,500	1,875
3	5,625	1,406
4	4,219	1,055
5	3,164	791
6	2,373	593
7	1,780	445
8	1,335	334
9	1,001	250
10	751	188

This method relies upon a percentage for the accelerated balance calculation. Given the percentage, we can replace the statement in line 540 of Fig. 4.10(C) with line 575, as follows:

575   LET A2 = P*A1

To be exact, the value of P should be obtained from the formula below:

$$P = 1 - \text{Yth root of } (S/C)$$

Recall that S and C are the salvage cost and original cost, respectively.

This method would be simple to calculate by hand if the Yth root calculation were not a problem. Often the value of P is arbitrarily chosen at 15 or 25 percent to avoid the difficult root extraction.

In either event, the Declining Balance method fails to give desirable results when the salvage value is zero. In this case, other methods should be applied.

How to Avoid Broken Programs

We have proposed several methods of avoiding program bugs. These methods are basically oriented toward the programmer rather than the user of a system. Briefly, the following techniques are recommended:

1. Instrument programs with probes
2. Use of menu programming
3. Programs written with an eye to their being read by others
4. Use of structuring concepts such as top-down refinement and the Boehm-Jacopini Result

Other precautions that can be taken are independent of the personal computing system. Such precautions are important to users regardless of the computer employed. They have been developed by business people to overcome errors that inevitably creep into any procedure for doing business. In particular, accountants have developed a technique called the *audit trail.*

The audit trail is valuable for the following purposes:

1. Error checking
2. Legal requirements
3. Validation by accountants
4. Data reconstruction procedures

The simplest audit trail is called the *backup procedure.* A backup procedure periodically prints all data on a sheet of paper called a *listing.* The listing is used as a permanent record of the activity (at a given point in time) of the company, computer, or personnel. The listing can be used to check errors, satisfy legal requirements, as validation by accountants, and for reconstruction of the data in the event of their loss.

The most critical area of data processing is the maintenance of files. A *file dump* is one way to produce an audit trail listing for a personal computer with tape or diskette. The file is a segment, or segments, of a tape or diskette containing records of information. When these records are modified, the computer system must indicate the fact that a modification has taken place by marking each modified record. This process is called *signing the record.* The signature audit trail in common use today writes the date of last modification in each record.

Figure 4.11 shows a before-and-after picture of a record that was marked by being signed with the date of modification. In this example, BALANCE was changed to reflect a payment on December 2, 1976 for the entry, "15660 BARNES." Hereafter, when a file dump is performed, the resulting listing will contain only those records that were signed since the previous file dump.

The audit trail procedure is used to catch errors, reconstruct lost files, and aid in the overall operation of a system. It is oriented toward assisting the people who will use the personal computer rather than those who program the system.

The audit trail is used in file structures rather than in program structures. For this reason, we must understand various file structures and how they work. In the following section, we present a brief introduction to file structures that will help you to understand the examples in subsequent chapters.

Acct. No.	Name	Balance	Signature		
11052	LEWIS	15.95	10	05	76
15660	BARNES	75.00	07	01	76
28553	TERRELL	00.00	01	10	77

(A)

Acct. No.	Name	Balance	Signature		
11052	LEWIS	15.95	10	05	76
15660	BARNES	00.00	12	02	76 ← Modify date
28553	TERRELL	00.00	01	10	77

(B)

Fig. 4.11   Signature audit trail for a file record: (A) Before, and (B) After

Files and Profiles

A *file* is a collection of records. A *record* is a collection of fields. A *field* is one or more *values*. Each value of a field is obtained from a variable. Thus, when writing a record in BASIC with fields A, B, and C, we would use the following statement:

PRINT   #S, A, B, C

Files are organized in one of several ways. The simplest structures are illustrated in Fig. 4.12. Study the examples of Fig. 4.11(A) in their file-structured form of Fig. 4.12, and notice the differences.

A *sequential file* is a storage structure in which every record is stored one after the other. Additions to the file are allowed only at its end. We can add a record 4 to the file of Fig. 4.12(A), but only at the end, as shown, not arbitrarily as in Fig. 4.12(B). A sequential file *must* be used in tape systems and is frequently used in disk systems because of its simplicity.

A *random file* is a structure that allows placement of each record in any (random) fashion. For example, Figure 4.12(B) shows one way the records of Fig. 4.11(A) might appear if stored on a random access diskette. Each record is retrieved by specifying a record number. The advantages of this organization are speed and directness. Random files are useful in diskette systems.

An *indexed file* is a collection of two or more subfiles. The *index subfile* contains a field from each record that uniquely identifies the record. The unique field is called a *key*. The key is stored in the index subfile along with a number that "points to" the complete record. The

(A) Sequential:

Record 1:	11052	LEWIS	15.95	100576
Record 2:	15660	BARNES	75.00	070176
Record 3:	28553	TERRELL	00.00	011077
Record 4:				

(B) Random:

Record 1:	11052	LEWIS	15.95	100576
Record 4:				
Record 3:	28553	TERRELL	00.00	011077
Record 2:	15660	BARNES	75.00	070176

(C) Indexed:

Index			*Master*				
Record 1:	11052	2	Record 1:	28553	TERRELL	00.00	011077
Record 2:	15660	3	Record 2:	11052	LEWIS	15.95	100576
Record 3:	28553	1	Record 3:	15660	BARNES	75.00	070176

Fig. 4.12   Organization of files

master subfile contains all complete records. It is usually stored as a random file. Figure 4.12(C) illustrates the two subfiles of an indexed structure. Note that each entry in the index subfile also contains a number corresponding to the record number in the master subfile. This number is called a *pointer.*

An indexed file structure may also have more than one index subfile. Each index subfile may contain a separate field which uniquely identifies each record. This organization enables the system to find the exact record desired in several different ways. For example, the records of Fig. 4.12(C) could be indexed by way of ACCT. NO., NAME, and any other field as long as the field remains unique to each record.

The concept of files and how to use them will be examined in greater detail in examples to follow. In the next section of this chapter, we will summarize the important points in programming.

Summary of Software Practice

We have now learned many of the basic concepts in programming. These concepts have evolved over the years because of their importance, but success as a programmer may be elusive even though the ideas are well understood. The reason for this disheartening fact is that programming is an art form. As with any art form, there are many of us who can never be one of its artists. Many others will be able to apply these techniques to their own situation, however, and become successful personal computer owners.

Chapter Five

Mr. J. and the Savings and Loan

"He roared past the speeding auto and before the riders could do anything about it he had smashed his fist into the engine. The car came to a metal-wrenching halt along the dusty country road. As it coasted to a complete stop, it nearly slid into a telephone pole standing in a ditch. In the process, the auto scraped a football field of blackberry bushes from the roadside and left a cloud of dust behind. Then he tore off the door. . . ."

Sitting in front of my family's new TV watching Superman mesmerized me as a child. We were the first in our neighborhood to own a TV, and thinking back about it now, I realize it must have looked strange in our house. There it was, a gigantic eye next to the RCA dog and mother's hanging laundry.

I guess our new TV wasn't as impressive to me as it was to my parents. After all, they grew up with out-houses and wood cook stoves. Now my kids are telling me that man can go to the moon and every office will be computer-controlled in a few more years. I'm not going to worry about it in my lifetime.

J. Henry Wendover, President,
Wendover Trucking Co., 1967

In this chapter and the next four, we are going to study detailed case histories of personal computing applications. Each one of the applications was chosen to demonstrate a feature of personal computing that can be applied to other situations. Taken together, these examples span the variety of techniques you will need to know for programming most applications that may arise in a home, office, or business.

Put Your Computer Where Your Money Is

Mr. J. comes from a wealthy East Coast family. His clan history can be traced all the way back to early American times. His great-great-great-grandfather was hanged by the British during the Revolutionary

War. The family was less proud of the cause of the hanging, which was for stealing horses, but nonetheless, they had poise, style, and breeding.

The family wealth was passed on to Mr. J. and his cousins when they became stable enough to be trusted with it. For J., this meant the very early age of nineteen. You see, Mr. J. is not only wealthy, but he has a clever financial mind.

Mr. J. has a cousin who inherited his share of the wealth at twenty-nine, and even that was too early. Cousin K. quickly spent his share and is now recovering from his fast life in a New York rest home. Mr. J. is much too cautious to let that happen to him.

In the first quarter of 1961, Mr. J. invested in a small loan company. The company specialized in very big deals, like financing oil well exploration, pipelines, ship fleets, and aircraft factories. The small company became a large holding company by 1969. In the first quarter of 1970, the holdings of Mr. J. included a savings and loan company. In fact, not only did Mr. J. own one savings and loan office, he actually owned hundreds of them under the name, Foist Federal Savings and Loan Co. of Noo Yawk.

This chain of savings and loan offices is spread over nearly the entire continental United States. Each office is run by a manager and a staff of bookkeepers, clerks, and loan officers.

The major cost item in Mr. J.'s operation was paperwork. If he could successfully reduce this part of the business to a reasonable level, he could afford to lower interest rates on loans and become more competitive. Several years ago, Mr. J. hired a systems analyst to study the idea that computers could be used to reduce the burden of paper work.

The systems analyst proceeded to design a system that initially included a central time-shared computer, telephone lines to each office, and a data-processing staff, as shown in Fig. 5.1.

The centralized system of Fig. 5.1 was implemented in 1968. The concept was advanced for its time because other savings and loan companies were slow to accept the idea of data processing with computers.

The time-sharing system cost Mr. J. ten million dollars. The programmers and other technical experts in the data-processing staff also cost the company millions of dollars each year, but they paid for themselves in saved paperwork.

By 1976, the system of Fig. 5.1 had been paid for by tax investment credits and reduced paperwork. The data-processing staff had completed their work, and the system was operating without much intervention. In fact, the only expense incurred by the paid-for system was the cost in maintenance and the data-processing staff salaries.

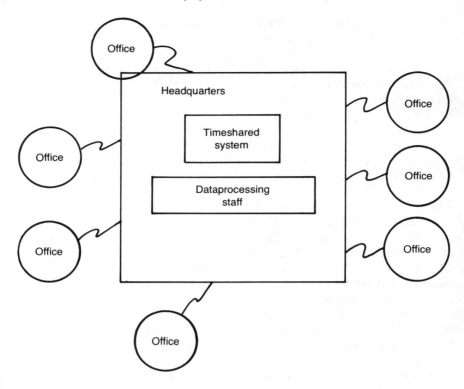

Fig. 5.1   The Savings and Loan time-shared system

The data-processing staff began pressing Mr. J. and the board of directors for a new budget. The new budget was to be used to pay for a "bigger and better" central system. The cost would be fantastic, but no other savings and loan company would have such a sophisticated system.

The board convened to discuss the proposal. Mr. J. made sure everyone present understood that he wanted the best possible system for their chain of offices. Mr. Peabody, Vice President of Finance, wanted to know how the new system would be financed. Mr. Jackson, Vice President of Operations, wanted to know how everyone in the company was going to learn how to handle a new system. Mr. Groaner complained that the computerization of office procedure was destroying customer relations. He wanted justification of the proposed system on the basis of human interaction.

Mr. J. was startled by the response. Apparently, the board had very real concerns about modernization. Such reactionism was out of proportion to the problem. There was a clear case of need, and the solution was obvious. Or was it?

The heated debate continued into the early morning hours. In the final round, the board agreed to hire a data-processing consultant to study the needs of the company and make recommendations. Mr. J. had held exactly this same kind of meeting years ago, and it resulted in the finest time-sharing system in the business. With a concealed smile he closed the present meeting, leaving everyone satisfied that a consultant would yield an answer. He would satisfy his board members and get the newer and bigger system, too.

RULE: POCKET CALCULATORS EXPAND TO FILL THE OFFICE

Hank had had twenty years in the data-processing business. The last five years had been spent consulting for companies like Mr. J.'s FFSLNY. So when he began studying the operations of FFSLNY he was surprised at his findings.

Most of the savings and loan offices were bogged down with hand calculations. Nearly every loan officer and office manager had a pocket calculator that was used as often as possible. The time-sharing terminal was avoided even though it could be used to perform the calculations being done by slower methods. Hank set about to find why the personnel were failing to take advantage of their powerful system. His findings were the following:

1. The terminal was complicated to use and the manuals difficult to read.
2. The telephone lines connecting each terminal to the central system were busy or inoperative much of the time. Whenever a clerk needed an answer, the system was slow to respond.
3. Most of the calculations that needed to be done were payments and payment schedules. These could be done by pocket calculators, even though the calculators were much slower.

By visiting several offices, Hank also discovered that the central computer was overburdened with trivial calculations. The result was poor performance and dissatisfaction. In addition, Hank could see no useful purpose in centralizing, because each savings and loan operated independently 95 percent of the time. This led Hank to recommend a dispersed system of personal computers as the solution.

Problem: How to Minimize Time, Maximize Service

The basic problem confronted by the savings and loan people was quite obvious to everyone but the board of directors and Mr. J. Therefore, Hank, the consultant, requested the board to visit one of their offices and see what happened when they tried to take out a loan.

Hank posed as a loan applicant while the corporation officers watched. The first step, of course, was to fill out an application form and a long financial statement. The statement and application were inspected by a receptionist, and after waiting several minutes, Hank was asked to step inside a booth along with a loan officer. The officer asked Hank the same questions that were answered in the application form and financial statement.

The corporate officers became impatient at this point and stepped in to save Hank. The loan officer immediately became excited when he realized that he was dealing with VIPs. In rapid succession, the application was approved, the financial statement cast aside, and Hank was asked how much he wanted to borrow.

"I don't exactly know, Mr. Murphy," Hank calmly replied. "I thought about $10,000, but what is your interest rate?"

"Is this a housing loan, business loan, or what?," the nervous officer asked. "How long would you want to keep the money?"

Hank was amused. "Let us assume this is a home loan, and I want to take the maximum time to repay it. I'd like to see how long it takes you to compute the payments, a schedule for the next five years, say, and how much interest I'll have to pay." The loan officer squirmed in his chair.

"Well now, we could make a five-year loan of $10,000 at an 8.75 percent annual rate of interest. If you made monthly payments, each payment would be, ah, let's see, about. . . . Just a moment, please." The loan officer opened a drawer in his desk and pulled out a pocket-sized book. He fumbled through the pages and once in a while looked nervously at the corporate officers standing by. Overcoming his confusion he said, "Oh yes, we can do that for, let's see, 8.25, ah, 8.50, yes, 8.75 percent is $198.50 per month."

The loan officer didn't realize that he had made an error in his monthly payment calculation. But Hank wasn't through tormenting him yet. "Suppose interest rates go up to 10.25 percent tomorrow. What would I expect to pay then?"

The loan officer rapidly looked in his book for a column with entries for 10.25 percent in it. Astounded, he realized that the entries stopped at 10.00 percent. Unwilling to give up in front of the VIPs, the loan officer triumphantly pulled a gleaming pocket calculator from his top drawer and began to push buttons feverishly. After quite a display of pocket calculator wizardry, he came up with the breathless answer: "$185.38 for five years, sir."

Hank roared with laughter. "You mean it will cost me less to borrow at 10.25 percent than at 8.75 percent? I think I'll wait until your interest rates go up! Thank you for your help, Mr. Murphy. I've seen enough."

The observing board members had seen enough, also. They went away convinced that any data-processing improvements must attack the basic problem of service. They wanted to know how to minimize the delay imposed by a loan officer and his pocket calculator, while maximizing customer service.

The solution to their problem was conceived by Hank and presented to them at their next meeting.

Solution: The Mortgage Computer

Hank's recommendation to FFSLNY was to disperse personal computers to each of the savings and loan offices. The current system of time-shared terminals would be replaced by "intelligent terminals," as shown in Fig. 5.2. In this new dispersed system, the features of time-sharing are retained by connecting each personal computer (the intelligent terminal) to the central time-shared network in exactly the

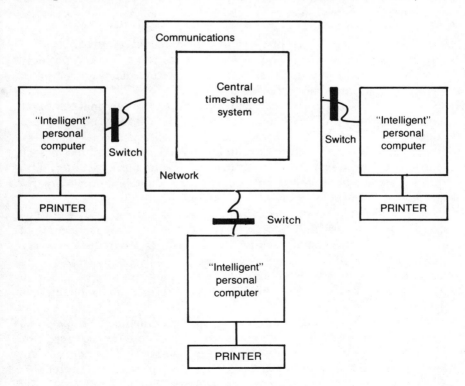

Fig. 5.2 Dispersed processing concept

same way as before. The difference is that each personal computer is now capable of two modes of operation:

1. Local processing
2. Remote processing

In the "local" mode of operation, the personal computers of Fig. 5.2 are independent of the communications network. This independence is obtained by turning the switch shown in the diagram of Fig. 5.2 to the "local" position. Each local processor operates exactly like any home computer, personal computer, or batch system.

Each personal computer in the FFSLNY computer system is connected to a printer. The configuration is as follows:

1. An 8 KB main memory processor
2. A 30-cps character printer with quality print font
3. A simple-to-use CRT/keyboard.

This configuration is powerful enough to do the computations that Mr. Murphy stumbled over. What is more, the printer is useful for generating a payment schedule including all of the information desired by a customer.

In the "remote" mode of operation, the personal computer becomes an "intelligent" terminal. The switch is set to the "remote" position, and the personal computer communicates with the corporate computer as if it were a time-sharing terminal.

Hank's design has an additional bonus. Since the personal computer is used in the local mode most of the time, there is no need for communication with the central machine except on special occasions. Before the dispersed concept was implemented, each terminal in each loan office had to be constantly connected to the main computer. This meant leasing a dedicated telephone line from the telephone company, and leased lines (point-to-point) are expensive.

The dispersed system requires connection by way of a telephone line for only a few minutes each day—at the beginning and end of the day when the system is used to get reports from the corporate office. It is much less expensive to use a regular dial telephone to accomplish this task even though the call is long distance. The leased line was removed and replaced by a regular telephone, modem, and acoustic coupler.

The *acoustic coupler* and *modem* are attachments to a personal computer that allow it to be connected to a telephone receiver. The bits inside computer memory are converted to sound by the modem and transmitted through the acoustic coupler to another computer that is also equipped with a modem and coupler. For example, a "1" bit is a middle "C," whereas a "0" bit might be an "F flat."

The converted sound is transmitted over a *voice grade* line if the transmission speed is low (300 bps). The sound is transmitted over a *conditioned* telephone line if the transmission speed is high (2400 bps). We say that these transmission rates are 300 baud and 2400 baud, respectively. (The word "baud" is derived from a French engineer's name and is pronounced "bawd"). Another unit of transmission speed is the unit of frequency, called "Hertz."

The FFSLNY computer is a personal computer when operated in local mode and an intelligent time-sharing terminal when operated in remote mode. The savings in telephone bills alone end up saving the loan corporation more money than their investment in the extra computers.

Design of a Mortgage Program

A mortgage program must be able to compute the monthly payments on a loan, including the amount of principle and interest. All home buyers are painfully aware that early payments are mostly an interest fee and contribute very little toward repayment of the balance. As the remaining balance declines from month to month, the amount paid for interest declines. In short, the first monthly payment is mostly interest and the last monthly payment is mostly principle.

Let's take a simple example. Suppose you get a loan for one dollar for four months at ten percent monthly interest. The *simple interest* on one dollar for four months is forty cents.

Simple Interest = ($1.00)(10 %)(4 months) = $0.40

If we were to add the interest to the principle, the payoff would be $1.40. In four equal monthly installments, each payment would be $0.35. Unfortunately, this calculation does not meet the requirements.

The savings and loan company is legally required to collect interest only on money that is outstanding for the current month. The interest must be computed for only one month at a time, and only on the remaining balance. If we apply this logic to the four month loan of one dollar at 10 percent interest we get the following incorrect payment schedule.

Month	Payment	Balance	Interest
1	$0.35	$0.75	$0.10
2	$0.35	$0.47 1/2	$0.07 1/2
3	$0.35	$0.17 1/4	$0.04 3/4
4	$0.35	Overpayment of $0.19475	$0.01725
Totals	$1.40		$0.23975

The resulting overpayment of nearly 19 ½ cents is the amount saved by the borrower when the declining balance schedule is used instead of the simple interest schedule. The declining balance method requires compensation in the payment schedule for the reduced interest fee. In a sense, the overpayment of nearly 20 cents must be distributed over the payment period. The approximate adjustment of ²⁰/₄, or 5 cents, reduces each payment to 30 cents per month. The following improved payment schedule uses the declining interest method:

Month	Payment	Balance	Interest
1	30¢	80¢	10¢
2	30¢	58¢	8¢
3	30¢	34¢	6¢
4	37¢	00	3¢
Totals	$1.27		27¢

The declining balance method reduces the total interest fee to 27 cents as opposed to the simple interest payment plan of 40 cents. Notice that the calculations were rounded-off to the nearest cent. This introduces errors into the calculation such that the last payment had to be increased to 37 cents.

If we are to use a declining balance method instead of a simple interest method, how do we calculate the "correct" payment? Obviously we could perform a simple interest calculation as we did above and then adjust the payments by the amount of overpayment divided by the number of payments. This method requires repeated (two or more) calculations of the schedule of payments. Each recalculation is an improvement over the previous one, but still only an approximation. There must be a better way.

Actuarial scientists developed a formula long ago that provides a short-cut we can use to get the amount of payment immediately. This formula depends upon the following quantities:

i = Monthly interest rate as a fraction
A = Amount borrowed
M = Number of months to complete repayment
     of amount and interest
V = Amount of one dollar when compounded
     by adding monthly interest fees.
     $= (i + 1)^M$

With the first three quantities as inputs, we can calculate V as indicated and then obtain the payment value for each month:

P = monthly payment
   $= (iVA)/(V - 1)$

For example, in the previous four-month illustration,

$$i = 0.1 \text{ (10\% per month)}$$
$$A = 1.00 \text{ (one dollar)}$$
$$M = 4 \text{ (four months)}$$

Then

$$V = (1.1)^4 = (1.4641)$$

This results in the payment,

$$P = (0.1)(1.4641)(1.00)/(0.4641)$$
$$= 0.14641/0.4641$$
$$= 31.5¢$$

Using this new improved formula, we can now produce a schedule of payments to beat all others.

Month	Payment	Balance	Interest
1	31.5¢	78.5¢	10.0¢
2	31.5¢	54.9¢	7.9¢
3	31.5¢	28.8¢	5.5¢
4	31.7¢	00.0¢	2.9¢
Totals	$ 1.26		26¢

The result of using the actuarial formula is a very exact but not 100 percent accurate schedule of payments. The final payment is ballooned by 0.2 cents in order to yield a final balance of zero. The total interest fee is 26 instead of 27 cents, and the total repayment is $1.26.

With this knowledge of how mortgage repayments work, we are prepared to write a BASIC mortgage program for a personal computer.

Blueprinting the Solution

The mortgage program runs interactively, with the user selecting inputs from a menu and supplying data as prompted by the program. We will tailor the input to suit a home buyer. This type of mortgage means the following data must be input:

1. Purchase price
2. Percent financed
3. Interest rate
4. Repayment period
5. Insurance premium (monthly)
6. Home owners tax (monthly)

These values are used to compute the base monthly mortgage payment plus the insurance and tax payment. The total monthly payment is the sum of the base payment plus tax and insurance.

The mortgage program is expected to output the schedule of payments including a month-to-month listing of the remaining balance and interest payment. The schedule is actually a table showing values of

1. Month
2. Payment
3. Balance (without interest)
4. Principle paid
5. Interest paid

In addition, we must guarantee that the program works properly. For this guarantee we ask that probes be included in the final program. The values of various probes are also printed at the end of each computer run. These probes consist of cross-footings, each of which should sum to zero.

Probe No. 1 = (Repayment Period in Months)(Payment) −
              (Total Payments)
Probe No. 2 = (Amount Borrowed) − (Total Principle Paid)
Probe No. 3 = (Total Interest Paid) + (Total Principle Paid)
              − (Total Payments)

If these probes are significantly different from zero, the program is said to be incorrect. Actually, the probes measure the validity of the program and the accuracy of the computer. Therefore, the value obtained for each probe will represent a small amount of inevitable round-off error.

The $BLUE_0$ specification of Fig. 5.3(A) demonstrates an abstraction of the mortgage program. In this figure the system is actually a four- or five-part program. In part one, the inputs are obtained from the prompting menu. In part two, the formula for payment amount is computed, and in part three, the table headings are listed. The fourth segment specifies the heart of the mortgage calculations. Within this part, a *nested* fifth part is calculated. The nested loop, as it is called, performs the necessary arithmetic to produce entries for the schedule of payments table. Finally, the summary values, including probe values, are printed.

In Fig. 5.3(B), we have converted the $BLUE_0$ specification into a more detailed blueprint. The variables that must be manipulated are explained in complete detail. The inputs are clearly shown in step 3.1, but without the menu. In step 3.2, the annual percentage rate is converted into a monthly fraction by dividing by 1200. The value

(A) BLUE₀

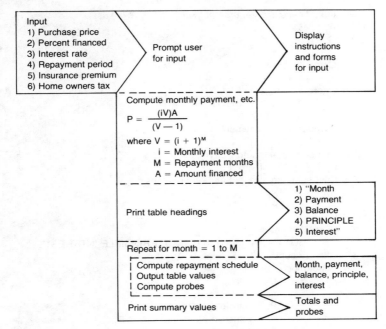

(B) BLUE₁
1. PROGRAM: Home Mortgage System for FFSLNY
2. DATA:

A = amount financed, initially unknown, also remaining balance

A_1 = purchase price, initially input

C = percent financed, initially input

I = monthly interest percent rate, initially input

I_1 = monthly interest rate as a fraction, initially unknown

I_2 = interest paid each month, initially unknown

I_3 = monthly home owners insurance premium, initially input

M = length of loan in months, initially input

D = down payment on loan, initially unknown

V = value of each dollar when finance charges for the term of the loan are added, initially unknown

P = monthly payment on loan, initially unknown

P_1 = remaining principle at each month, initially unknown

P_2 = total monthly payment including insurance and taxes, initially unknown

S_1 = sum paid in interest, initially zero

S_2 = sum paid in principle, initially zero

S_3 = sum paid in monthly payment, initially zero

J = month number, initially one

T = monthly tax, initially input

$X_1 = X_2 = X_3$ = probes, initially unknown

Fig. 5.3 Blueprints for the mortgage payment system

3. STEPS:

    3.1 Input financial data, prompt user

        A_1 M

        C I_3

        I   T

    3.2 Compute monthly payment

$$P = A * (I_1 * V)/(V - 1)$$

where $V = (I_1 + 1)^M$

        $A = C * A_1/100.00$

        $I_1 = I/1200.0$

    3.3 Compute down payment

$$D = (100.00 - C) * A_1$$

    3.4 Compute total monthly payment

$$P_2 = P + I_3 + T$$

    3.5 Print summary of input and other values

        A_1 P_2

        A   P

        I_1

    3.6 Print table headings

        "MONTH PAYMENT BALANCE PRINCIPLE INTEREST"

    3.7 Initialize sums, $S_1 = S_2 = S_3 = 0$

    3.8 Repeat loop For J = 1 to M

        3.8.1 Compute

           I_2 = interest = $I_1 * A$

           P_2 = principle = $P - I_2$

           A = remaining balance = $A - P_1$

        3.8.2 Compute probes

           S_1 = sum of I_2 = $S_1 + I_2$

           S_2 = sum of P_1 = $S_2 + P_1$

           S_3 = sum of P = $S_3 + P$

        3.8.3 Print table entry

           J, P, A, P_1, I_2

    3.9 Compute probes

        $X_1 = M * P - S$ (should be 0.0)

        $X_2 = A - S_2$ (should be 0.0)

        $X_3 = S_1 + S_2 - S_3$ (should be 0.0)

    3.10 Print summary values and probe values

        "Total Interest," S_1

        "Total Principle," S_2

        "Total Payments," S_3

        "Payment Probe (0.0)," X_1

        "Balance Probe (0.0)," X_2

        "Crossfooting Check (0.0)," X_3

    3.11 Stop

(C) BLUE$_2$

```
1 REM  ***********************************************************
2 REM
3 REM      HOME MORTGAGE SYSTEM FOR FFSLNY COMPANY
4 REM            COPYRIGHT 1977
5 REM
7 REM  ***********************************************************
```

Fig. 5.3 Continued

```
8 DIM Y$[3]
10 PRINT "PURCHASE PRICE (DOLLARS AND CENTS) : $";
15 INPUT A1
16 PRINT "PER CENT FINANCED (%)                  : ";
17 INPUT C
20 PRINT "AMOUNT OF INTEREST (PER CENT) RATE : ";
25 INPUT I
30 PRINT "TERM (MONTHS)                         : ";
35 INPUT M
36 PRINT "AMOUNT OF INSURANCE PER MONTH        : $";
37 INPUT I3
38 PRINT "AMOUNT OF TAXES PER MONTH            : $";
39 INPUT T
40 REM ******************************************************************
41 LET I1=I/1200.000000
42 LET D=(100.00-C)*A1
43 LET A=C*A1/100.00000
50 LET V=(1.0000000+I1).^M
60 LET P=(I1*V)/(V-1.0000000)*A
61 LET X2=A
62 LET P2=P+I3+T
63 PRINT#4, "PURCHASE PRICE        : $", A1
64 PRINT#4, "LOAN AMOUNT           : $", A
65 PRINT#4, "INTEREST RATE/MONTH:    ", I1
66 PRINT#4, "MONTHLY PAYMENT       : $", P2
67 PRINT#4, "PAID   TO PRINCIPLE   : $", P
68 PRINT#4
69 PRINT#4, "MONTH    PAYMENT    BALANCE", TAB(33), "PRINCIPLE       INTEREST"
70 PRINT#4, "_____"
71 LET S1=0
72 LET S2=0
73 LET S3=0
75 REM***************************************************************
76 FOR J=1 TO M
80 LET I2=I1*A
90 LET P1=P-I2
100 LET A=A-P1
110 LET S1=S1+I2
120 LET S2=S2+P1
130 LET S3=S3+P
132 IF A>0.00 THEN 140
134 LET A=0.00
140 PRINT#4, J, TAB(9), P, TAB(22), A, TAB(35), P1, TAB(48), I2
150 REM***************************************************************
151 REM
152 REM    OUTPUT SCHEDULE OF PAYMENTS
153 REM
154 REM***************************************************************
155 NEXT J
158 PRINT#4, "_____"
159 PRINT#4
160 PRINT#4, "TOTAL INTEREST PAID      : $", S1
162 PRINT#4, "TOTAL PRINCIPLE PAID     : $", S2
164 PRINT#4, "TOTAL PAYMENTS           : $", S3
170 LET X1=M*P-S3
180 LET X2=X2-S2
185 LET X3=S1+S2-S3
190 PRINT#4, "PROBE 1 : ", X1
192 PRINT#4, "PROBE 2 : ", X2
194 PRINT#4, "PROBE 3 : ", X3
200 PRINT "DO YOU WANT TO STOP ?";
202 INPUT Y$
205 IF Y$="NO" THEN 10
210 STOP
```

Fig. 5.3 Continued

of V is obtained by raising the monthly interest fraction, plus one, to the Mth power.

In steps 3.3 and 3.4, we specify the amount to be financed and the total monthly payment, including taxes and insurance. These values are output, along with the input values (for accuracy checking), in step 3.5. We are careful to initialize the totals used to compute cross-footings in step 3.7. Finally, the repeat loop is used in step 3.8 to generate each entry in the schedule of payments.

The nested loop contains three sections, as shown by segments 3.8.1, 3.8.2, and 3.8.3 of Fig. 5.3(B). In the first segment, the interest payment I_2, principal payment P_1, and declining balance are computed in proper order. The next segment produces values to be used in cross-footing and calculation of validation probes. Finally, the table entries are printed.

In section 3.9 of the BLUE$_1$ language program, each probe is tallied for final output. In each case, the sums are expected to be zero, but watch what happens in the following sample calculations.

Translating Blueprints to Code

The final version of the mortgage system is blueprinted in BASIC for a particular personal computer. In the program of Fig. 5.3(C), we used a dialect of BASIC with a few minor differences that may cause trouble when running this program on another personal computer. These differences will be pointed out as we analyze the program.

In line 8, the DIM statement is used to inform the BASIC interpreter that we intend to use Y$ as a string variable with a maximum of three characters allowed. Thus, if Y$ = "YES" or if Y$ = "NO," the length stated in DIM will suffice to store both strings.

In statements 10 through 39, the program displays a menu, and the user is prompted to give input. For example, if we were to reproduce the four-month schedule of payments shown earlier for a $1 loan, the menu and the input would look as follows (where values in italics are provided by the user).

PURCHASE PRICE (DOLLARS AND CENTS)	:	$ *1.00*
PERCENT FINANCED(%)	:	*100*
AMOUNT OF INTEREST (%) RATE	:	*120*
TERM (MONTHS)	:	*4*
AMOUNT OF INSURANCE PER MONTH	:	*$0.00*
AMOUNT OF TAXES PER MONTH	:	*$0.00*

In lines 41 through 62, the BASIC program carries out the calculations specified in sections 3.2 through 3.4 of the BLUE$_1$ specification of Fig. 5.3(B). Notice, however, that the order in which the calculations are performed has been changed. When using top-down refinement, the increased level of detail in a subsequent refinement often means rearranging the order of actual statements.

In line 41, we convert I from annual percent to a monthly fraction. In lines 42 and 43, the loan amount is computed based upon the percent to be financed. (In this version of the program, an unnecessary calculation has been included; can you find it?) The value of a dollar, compounded for M months at $I_1 * 100$ percent per month is computed in line 50 by raising $(1 + I_1)$ to the M th power. Notice the use of a "$\wedge$" character to show exponentiation. This value is then applied in line 60 to obtain the base monthly payment. In line 61, we save the value A in probe X_2. During the calculation of the schedule, the declining balance, A, will vary. Therefore, X_2 will hold the initial declining balance for later reference. The total monthly payment is computed in line 62.

The output of lines 63 through 70 yields summary information, table headings, and formatting for a readable output. Here is where we will encounter some differences in BASIC dialects. We have used PRINT #4 to indicate output to a character printer. In fact, as you can see, the character printer is a dot-matrix printer. This particular personal computer allocates unit #4 as the system printer.

In lines 71 to 73, the cross-footing totals are initialized to zero.

In lines 76 to 155, the loop shown in $BLUE_0$ and $BLUE_1$ is defined. The month J is used as a loop counter. First, the interest fee on the remaining balance A is computed. Then the principal paid is computed by subtracting the interest fee from the monthly base payment, line 90. Finally, the declining balance owed is computed by subtracting the principal payment from the current balance. The cross-footing totals are summed in lines 110 to 130.

Lines 132 and 134 are additions to the blueprints for the mortgage program. They are inserted to guarantee that the last payment produces a zero declining balance. Actually, the last balance will be a hair off due to round-off error. The final balance would be some nonzero balance without lines 132 and 134. Customers become upset if they discover that they still owe a few pennies after their last payment. To compensate for the psychology of humans, the savings and loan will either adjust the final balance as shown here, or they will adjust the final payment to compensate for round-off.

Line 140 is a printer output statement. Unit #4 is an 80-column, bidirectional printer that sprays dot-matrix characters at a rate of 80 cps. The TAB control function moves the printer head to columns 9, 22, 35, and 48, respectively, as indicated. Other personal computers may also perform the tab function, but a different dialect of BASIC may be employed.

The loop is terminated in line 155. In line 159, the single PRINT statement produces a blank line (double space) to set off the schedule from the summary information printed in lines 160 and 164.

The probes used as an accuracy check and to validate the program itself are computed in lines 170 to 185. They are output in lines 190 to 194.

In lines 200 and 202, we use Y$ to input a YES or NO. This allows us to run the program a second time by responding "NO" to the question. Otherwise, the program terminates with line 210.

This program is a direct result of the top-down refinement process. Beginning with $BLUE_0$ and working toward $BLUE_2$ is a two-step process involving two levels of abstraction. The author must confess, however, that the actual design and development process used to arrive at the final program took several passes. The top-down method was used iteratively. First, an early version of $BLUE_0$ and $BLUE_1$ was sketched. The early sketches were modified several times while attempting to write the BASIC program. After several trials, the BASIC program was tested and additional modifications made to the final blueprints.

The actual "errors" and modifications made during the many iterations are listed below:

1. Forgetting to DIM Y$ in line 8

2. Improper calculations in lines 41 to 62

3. Disorganized formatting and output spacing in all PRINT #4 statements, especially in line 69

4. Failure to initialize sums in lines 71 to 73

5. Incorrect order of calculations in lines 80 through 100

6. Oversight concerning round-off errors, which were more than originally thought. This meant adding lines 132 and 134.

7. Line 180 was originally incorrect because the first version used $X_2 = A - S_2$ instead. This meant adding line 61.

This is the only time the author will admit to imperfection. Note, however, that the actual development time for this program was many hours. The final version in Fig. 5.3(C) is not yet perfect, but it does work. Approximately a dozen test runs were made from beginning to end.

Testing the Mortgage Program

The mortgage program was developed over a period of several days, involving over a dozen sample runs and many modifications as pointed out before. Exactly how can we guarantee that the final product is correct? What do we mean by correct?

The BASIC program of Fig. 5.3(C) is only partially correct. It will fail if we do any of the following:
1. Input negative or zero values
2. Input numbers that are too large
3. Ask for a payment schedule that is too long, for example, 5000 months

In other words, the program is frail because we did not include enough checks in it. We could, for example, test every input value and guarantee it before continuing with the calculations. This alteration would double the size of the program but would probably be worth the added effort.

Printing from a Test Case

Suppose we begin testing the program using familiar data. The table of section B is a good place to begin. Can the program reproduce the four-month payment schedule of a $1 loan at 120 percent annual interest rate? Consider Fig. 5.4.

```
PURCHASE PRICE      : $        1
LOAN AMOUNT         : $        1
INTEREST RATE/MONTH:          .1
MONTHLY PAYMENT     : $        .315471
PAID TO PRINCIPLE   : $        .315471

MONTH   PAYMENT   BALANCE       PRINCIPLE      INTEREST
-----------------------------------------------------------------
1       .315471   .784529       .215471        .1
2       .315471   .54751        .237019        7.84529E-2
3       .315471   .28679        .26072         5.4751E-2
4       .315471   0             .286793        2.8679E-2
-----------------------------------------------------------------

TOTAL INTEREST PAID    : $    .261883
TOTAL PRINCIPLE PAID   : $    1
TOTAL PAYMENTS         : $    1.26189
PROBE 1 :          0
PROBE 2 :          -3.09944E-6
PROBE 3 :          0
```

Fig. 5.4 Printed output from mortgage program: Amount of purchase, $1.00; on 100 percent loan; 120 percent annual interest rate; for four months; no insurance or taxes

The output of Fig. 5.4 illustrates a typical run. The purchase price and amount of loan are each one dollar. Since a 120 percent annual interest rate was input, the monthly rate is 10 percent. The monthly payments are 31.5¢ each, just as we calculated in the second section of this chapter. In fact, we obtain the same results with the personal computer as we did by hand, except for the additional round-off. This round-off is indicated by probe 2 in Fig. 5.4.

The output of Fig. 5.4 is messy. We see scientific notation being used. For example, $-3.09944E-6$ stands for -0.00000309944 because the $E-6$ means to place the decimal point six digits to the left of where it was printed. Notice how much more compact the E notation is, even though it may be cryptic. We could also express 1,000,000 more compactly by writing it as $1.0E+6$. This saves space and makes it easier to read output once the notation is mastered.

In business, calculations must be in dollars and cents. Therefore only two decimal fraction digits are really needed. We can limit the output to dollars and cents in some dialects of BASIC that permit the PRINT USING statement. Thus, for example, if we replaced the PRINT statements in the mortgage program with:

192　　PRINT #4 USING 1000, X 2
1000　　"PROBE 2:" ###.##

The USING statement directs the BASIC interpreter to use statement 1000 as a pattern for the output. The # characters are replaced by digits, and the decimal point is forced into a "dollars and cents" position.

Once we are satisfied with the preliminary test based upon familiar data, we can perform a "reasonableness test." This test is made by using realistic data and examining the output to see if it looks reasonable.

The sample of Fig. 5.5 satisfies several reasonableness tests. It is reasonable to assume $80 interest on nearly a $10,000 loan for one month at 0.00833 interest rate. It is also reasonable, but unfortunate, to assume a total repayment of $11,151.70. The total principal paid is 19¢ above the amount financed, but this too is reasonable when round-off is considered. Finally, we see that the probes are as expected, including a check on round-off accuracy.

We can certify the mortgage program in the following way: "The mortgage program is verified for positive input data that is reasonably large and for output data that is reasonably small and accurate." Therefore, we are ready to accept the mortgage problem as a solved problem.

The mortgage program is saved on diskette or tape for use by the loan officers at the Foist Federal Savings and Loan of Noo Yawk. In fact, there is an end to the story.

Hank, the consultant, installed a prototype "intelligent terminal" in one of the FFSLNY loan offices. At first, everyone was skeptical of change, and Hank had to twist arms to get someone to be first.

The mortgage program was run for a few loan applications, and when the loan officer saw the printer at work, Hank's job was done.

```
PURCHASE PRICE     : $          12000
LOAN AMOUNT        : $          9600
INTEREST RATE/MONTH:            8.33333E-3
MONTHLY PAYMENT    : $          328.02
PAID  TO PRINCIPLE : $          309.77
```

MONTH	PAYMENT	BALANCE	PRINCIPLE	INTEREST
1	309.77	9370.23	229.77	80
2	309.77	9138.55	231.684	78.0853
3	309.77	8904.93	233.615	76.1546
4	309.77	8669.37	235.562	74.2078
5	309.77	8431.84	237.525	72.2447
6	309.77	8192.34	239.504	70.2654
7	309.77	7950.84	241.5	68.2695
8	309.77	7707.33	243.513	66.257
9	309.77	7461.79	245.542	64.2277
10	309.77	7214.2	247.588	62.1815
11	309.77	6964.55	249.651	60.1183
12	309.77	6712.81	251.732	58.0379
13	309.77	6458.98	253.83	55.9401
14	309.77	6203.04	255.945	53.8249
15	309.77	5944.96	258.078	51.692
16	309.77	5684.73	260.228	49.5413
17	309.77	5422.34	262.397	47.3728
18	309.77	5157.75	264.584	45.1861
19	309.77	4890.96	266.788	42.9813
20	309.77	4621.95	269.012	40.758
21	309.77	4350.7	271.253	38.5163
22	309.77	4077.19	273.514	36.2558
23	309.77	3801.39	275.793	33.9765
24	309.77	3523.3	278.091	31.6783
25	309.77	3242.89	280.409	29.3608
26	309.77	2960.15	282.746	27.0241
27	309.77	2675.04	285.102	24.6679
28	309.77	2387.57	287.478	22.292
29	309.77	2097.69	289.873	19.8964
30	309.77	1805.4	292.289	17.4808
31	309.77	1510.68	294.725	15.045
32	309.77	1213.5	297.181	12.589
33	309.77	913.842	299.657	10.1125
34	309.77	611.688	302.154	7.61535
35	309.77	307.016	304.672	5.0974
36	309.77	0	307.211	2.55846

```
TOTAL INTEREST PAID     : $    1551.51
TOTAL PRINCIPLE PAID    : $    9600.19
TOTAL PAYMENTS          : $    11151.7
PROBE 1 :        2.92969E-3
PROBE 2 :        -.195313
PROBE 3 :        1.95313E-3
```

Fig. 5.5 Printed output for mortgage program: Amount of purchase, $12,000; 80 percent loan; 10 percent annual interest; 36 months; $10.75 monthly insurance; and $7.50 taxes

Several months later, every branch office of FFSLNY installed one or more personal computers. Today, these machines are not only computing mortgage schedules, but doing nearly every kind of processing required in running a modern savings and loan company.

Mr. J. and the board were proud of themselves. They maintained their lead in the business by being first to accept the common computer age, and in addition, they were saving on overhead expenses. Together, Mr. J., Peabody, Jackson, and Groaner went to lunch knowing that they had done the correct thing.

Chapter Six

SENATOR B AND THE MAILING LIST

A young man set out to seek ultimate wisdom and knowledge. He searched the land from mountain to valley, north to south. Everywhere he went, he would ask the villagers, strangers, and kind people who offered him a place to sleep, "Who possesses the wisdom and knowledge of the world?" And the answer was always the same; the interrogated would hunch-up their shoulders and with a puzzled look exclaim, "We cannot help you."

The young man continued his quest for an answer, and as the years faded into history, he became an old man. In his travels he met nearly all of the people in his nation, and as he became known to them all, his reputation grew. He was considered a strange man at first, but as he grew wrinkled, bent, and gray, he gave the appearance of a sage. Everywhere he went, he asked, "Where can I find the wisest of them all, the source of all truth?" And the answers he received were all empty and without meaning.

The legend of the old man became known to every child, carpenter, brick mason, shopkeeper, and merchant in the country. Stories were told of the enlightening meetings with him, and people flocked to hear his tales of travel. He became the greatest of them all, and yet when he asked, "What is truth and beauty?," the only voice he heard was his own.

As told to me by Rubinsk Pontus, 1973

The Post Office and Disorder

Bertrand K. Gambit was born and raised in a logging town at the base of the Cascade Mountains. He was a good quarterback for the high school football team, and most people remember him as a tall, friendly kid who always had a girl friend.

The Oregon town that Bertrand grew up in was too small for his ambitions so when he turned eighteen, he left home. He still remembers how worried his sister looked when he jumped aboard a lumber train rolling down the tracks crossing Main Street. Sis waved goodbye and turned to run home and announce the bad news to their parents.

Bert spent the next ten years roaming around the country. He visited California, Colorado, Louisiana, and Arizona before returning. His travels were a good education for the jobs that lay in his future.

One day on Bourbon Street in New Orleans, Bertrand saw a personal computer taking pictures of tourists. He bought a cob of corn and a pint of wine and leaned against the old Bourbon Street building to take a look at the computer that was printing pictures.

An amazed crowd of people gathered around the personal computer. The system consisted of a video camera, a dot-matrix character printer, and a computer. Egotistical tourists would stand in front of a white screen while the camera scanned them, and, in turn, produced a picture by printing dark and light patterns on paper.

Bertrand looked closely at a picture being printed by the dot-matrix printer. The darkest areas consisted of "#" characters, while light areas were made of ";" and periods. The shades in between were constructed from other letters and characters; "M", "8", "=", and "−." Bertrand was amazed like everyone else.

Iberville St., Lake Ponchartrain, and the humidity of New Orleans lost its appeal after a few years, and Bertrand yearned for a change. So he returned to Oregon.

Bertrand was always known as a friendly kid. He had thousands of friends throughout Oregon, and his hobbies (flying, boating, mountain climbing) and business expanded his friendships. It was during a conversation with one of his flying companions that Bertrand first began thinking seriously about running for public office.

"Bert, you know we are going to have a problem on our hands here in Oregon if we don't do something about growth, pollution, and people," said Catfish Dave, a long-time complainer. "I mean, look at how much your own home town has changed in the last ten years."

"Yeah, well, what do you think anyone can do about it, Catfish?" Bertrand tried to sound concerned. His friend Catfish Dave was always talking about some kind of disorder.

"I been thinkin' it over, Bert, and I say you should run for senator and do something about it." He paused a moment as if to see what Bertrand's reaction would be, but then pressed on. "I am serious, Bert. You know enough people in Oregon to get elected without campaigning."

"And I suppose you want to be my campaign manager, Catfish," Bertrand laughed. "Haven't you got other things to do besides butt into politics, Dave?"

The weeks passed by, and Catfish kept reminding Bertrand of his idea. The two of them talked for many hours before Bertrand got serious about running for senator.

To make a short story of it, Bertrand eventually became a senator, and, incidentally, he accomplished this feat with the assistance of a personal computer. How the senator and a personal computer got together is the subject of the next section on postal service.

Rule: Mail Expands to Fill the Post Office

Senator-to-be Bertrand K. Gambit and his campaign manager Catfish Dave decided that their method of reaching voters would be through the mail. Brochures describing the senator's stand on pollution, expansion and growth of Oregon's industry, and population would be distributed by "mailers" sent to each registered voter.

The brochure would be an envelope-sized flyer with the name and address of the occupant on one side and the slogan "Keep Oregon Livable" on the other side.

Catfish Dave visited the local post office and learned that mailing rates would be very expensive unless the brochures were mailed in bulk. The bulk mailing rules specified that each bulk must contain at least two hundred brochures, and furthermore, all of the brochures must be put into order from small zip code value to large zip code value. Catfish could sense that this was going to be a very big job.

Problem: How to Minimize Cost, Maximize Service

The problem faced by Bertrand and Catfish was to sort the 50,000 letters into ascending zip code order to save money on postage. The mailing label would consist of other information as well. Sample labels for the senator and some of his friends are shown in Fig. 6.1(A). The result of ordering these labels is shown in the list of zip codes of Fig. 6.1(B).

Bertrand and Catfish were stunned by the job they faced. Then Bertrand remembered the picture-taking personal computer that he had seen in New Orleans. It gave him an idea.

"We can get a computer to do this work for us, Catfish!" Bertrand literally shouted. "I've got it."

"Yer gone stark," Catfish snapped. "What are you ravin', boy?"

Solution: Bulk Mailing

Bertrand and Catfish went shopping for a bulk mailing computer. They visited several computer shops in Portland and Eugene and learned all they could about personal computing. But they felt uncomfortable around computers, as it turned out, and they decided to take a second approach.

Next, they hired a volunteer who also worked as a programmer. The programmer, Fred Byte, was an enthusiastic supporter of Bertrand

(A) Three Labels

```
FILE :          MAILERS          FROM DEVICE :   1              LISTING
------------------------------------------------------------------
        Bert K. Gambit
        1451 Smithsonian C
        Sweetwater, Or.
         97350
        ----------------------------------------------
        Catfish Dave, J
        856 Harlan Dr.
        Horsefalls, Or.
         97832
        ----------------------------------------------
        Oziah Klampit
        97 Cliff Trails
        Rt. 2, Box 38, Or
         96101
        ----------------------------------------------
```

(B) Output from Sorting Labels of (A)

```
MERGE/SORT ROUTINE.
DATA :          1              =   97350
DATA :          2              =   97832
DATA :          3              =   96101
N =             3              PROBES......
PROBE 1 SHOULD BE             3            IS          3
PROBE 2 SHOULD BE             1            IS          1
PROBE 3 SHOULD BE             3            IS          3
PROBE 4 SHOULD BE             3            IS          3
PROBE 5 SHOULD BE 0.0, IS     0
   1            :             96101        3
   2            :             97350        1
   3            :             97832        2
END OF MERGE/SORT
```

Fig. 6.1 The mailing labels for Senator Gambit

and had grown up with the senator-to-be. Fred got even more excited about the possibility of working on the campaign as a programmer.

The three of them went to a nearby computer shop and after an hour or two left the shop with a box under Fred's arm. The personal computer they had purchased consisted of the following items:

1. A 16KB memory processor with its own keyboard, packaged in one box
2. An interface to make the keyboard and processor work with an ordinary television set (as the output device for an operator)
3. An interface to make two ordinary cassette tape recorders work with the processor as a mass storage medium (this gave the system capability for storing 50,000 mailing labels)
4. A small printer that would be used to print mailing labels in zip code order

The system was installed in Fred's home so that he could write the programs needed to do the mailing. All Fred had to do was program the machine to turn it into a mailing list computer.

The Mailing List Computer

Fred Byte was an experienced computer programmer, but he had never used a personal computer before. It took him several hours to understand what he had to do. After some study, though, Fred knew exactly what had to be done.

One of Fred's chores was to discover how BASIC handles *array* information. An array is a collection of one or more values that are organized into a single block called the *array name* and accessed by a *subscript variable*. The size of an array is given in a DIM statement in BASIC:

10   DIM A(10), Y$(3)

In this example, the DIM statement tells the BASIC interpreter program that a block of ten values are reserved for array A, and a block of three characters is reserved for string array Y$. The maximum number of values stored in A will be ten numbers, while the maximum stored in Y$ will be three characters.

The values of an array are input simply by *indexing* their subscripts, as illustrated in the following segment of code.

```
1000   FOR I = 1 TO 10
1010   INPUT "ARRAY VALUE =," A(I)
1020   NEXT I
1025   RETURN
```

This example demonstrates the use of an INPUT statement that also displays a prompting message. This feature may not be allowed in some dialects of BASIC. The value of subscript I is computed with a FOR loop. This value is used to access the Ith element of array A.

Similarly, we can output arrays with a loop mechanism:

```
1050   FOR I = 1 TO 10
1060   PRINT I, A(I)
1070   NEXT I
1075   RETURN
```

Finally, we can search an array to find the value that matches some *search key* X, as follows:

```
1100   FOR I = 1 TO 10
1105   IF A(I) = X THEN 1200
1110   NEXT I
1120   PRINT "NOT FOUND"
1125   RETURN
1200   PRINT "FOUND AT SUBSCRIPT:", I
1205   RETURN
```

This segment of code looks for a value of A(I) that exactly equals the value of X. When found, the subscript corresponding with A(I) = X is printed. If not found, the message, "NOT FOUND" is printed.

Fred Byte also had to learn how to call *subroutines* in BASIC. A subroutine is a segment of code in BASIC that is executed exactly as if it were one line of BASIC code, even though it may consist of a dozen lines. Let us see how this is done.

Suppose that we want to use the three routines previously shown to demonstrate how to input, output, and search an array. We could insert these routines into every program that needs them, or we could use them over and over again with the GOSUB command.

```
750   REM INPUT ARRAY A
800   GOSUB 1000
850   REM OUTPUT ARRAY A
900   GOSUB 1050
950   REM SEARCH FOR X
955   INPUT "KEY:", X
960   GOSUB 1100
990   STOP
```

The GOSUB and array features of BASIC are rather standard. We will use them heavily in explaining Fred's mailing list program written for Senator Gambit.

Sorting by Selection

Fred's first attempt at sorting the zip codes for Senator Gambit worked fine when he tried it on ten numbers. We can see how it works by looking at the following example. Suppose we want to sort the numbers below:

$$L(1) = 3$$
$$L(2) = 1$$
$$L(3) = 2$$

First, we must invent a strategy. Fred's strategy is to search the list from L(1) to L(3) and determine which element is the largest. He

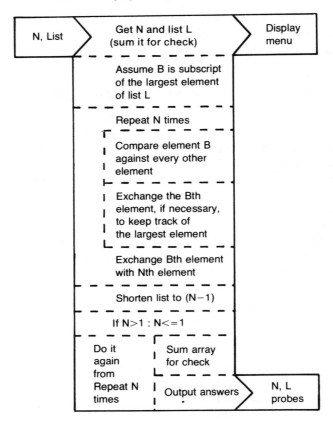

Fig. 6.2   BLUE₀ specification of selection sort package

then takes the largest (in this case 3) and exchanges it with the last element L(3). This exchange produces the partially ordered list below:

$$L(1) = 2$$
$$L(2) = 1$$
$$L(3) = 3$$

Since the largest number is in the final position of the array, the list can now be sorted from top to L(2). The value in L(3) never needs to be checked again because L(3) equals the largest value in the list.

The next pass over L(1) and L(2) produces the sublist below.

$$L(1) = 1$$
$$L(2) = 2$$

A subsequent pass over L(1) alone produces a sublist, as shown:

$$L(1) = 1$$

The complete list is now in order because every sublist is in order. This method is often called *selection sort* because of the method of selecting the largest element. It is also sometimes called *exchange sort* because after each pass, we exchange the largest element with the last element in each sublist.

The blueprints for this method are illustrated in Figs. 6.2 and 6.3. We have removed BLUE$_1$ (pseudo code) from this set of specifi-

```
1000 REM ***********************************************************
1001 REM                   SELECTION    SORT
1002 REM                    COPYWRITE 1977
1003 REM ***********************************************************
1004 REM
1005 DIM L[25]
1006 REM SET PROBE SUM TO ZERO, INITIALLY
1007 LET P0=0
1008 REM
1009 REM GET DATA
1010 PRINT "SELECTION SORT."
1011 PRINT "INPUT N="; INPUT N
1012 LET M=N
1013 FOR I=1 TO N
1015 PRINT I, " : "; INPUT L[I]
1017 LET P0=P0+L[I]
1018 NEXT I
1019 REM
1020 REM GET BIGGEST NUMBER.
1022 LET B=1
1024 FOR I=1 TO N
1026 IF L[B]>L[I] THEN 1030
1028 LET B=I
1030 NEXT I
1031 REM
1032 REM    EXCHANGE BIGGEST FOR LAST.
1034 LET T=L[N]
1036 LET L[N]=L[B]
1038 LET L[B]=T
1039 REM
1040 REM   SHORTEN LIST
1042 LET N=N-1
1044 REM
1049 REM    DONE ?
1050 IF N>1 THEN 1022
1052 REM   CHECK PROBE
1055 FOR I=1 TO M
1057 LET P0=P0-L[I]
1059 NEXT I
1060 REM
1061 REM    OUTPUT
1063 PRINT#4, "  I   :       L(I)"
1065 FOR I=1 TO M
1067 PRINT#4, TAB(2), I, TAB(6), ": ", TAB(10), L[I]
1068 NEXT I
1069 PRINT#4
1070 PRINT#4, "     PROBE SHOULD BE 0.0=", P0
1075 RETURN
```

Fig. 6.3 BLUE$_2$ specification of selection sort

```
 I   :      L(I)
 1   :     -8.1
 2   :     -7.5
 3   :     -3.5
 4   :      3.6
 5   :      5
 6   :      7.5
 7   :      7.5
 8   :      7.5
 9   :     10.5

     PROBE SHOULD BE 0.0=          3.8147E-6
```

Fig. 6.4   Sample output from selection sort

cations because of this problem's simplicity. The steps shown in Fig. 6.3 are analyzed with the assistance of the sample data shown sorted in Fig. 6.4. These data were input as follows:

N = 9
Data = 10.5, −8.1, −3.5, 7.5, 5.0, 7.5, 3.6, 7.5, −7.5

We can follow the first pass of the program of Fig. 6.3 by assuming this input.

Line 1012 is used to save the value N = 9 for later use (see lines 1055 to 1059 and 1065 to 1068). The value stored in N will be decreased by one after each pass over the original array.

In line 1015, we use a short-cut method of writing BASIC statements. The semicolon separates the PRINT and INPUT commands and serves to compress the code. The summation in line 1017 will be used for the check sum probe. Before the sort takes place, PØ will be the sum of elements in L; after the array is sorted, PØ will be reduced by the amount of the new array (see lines 1055 to 1059). Hence, if both sums are the same, we certify that the program is correct.

The central part of the selection sort is in lines 1022 through 1050. Here, the subscript B is used to indicate the subscript of the largest element in L. We start out by assuming that B equals one, and then change B whenever a larger element is discovered (see lines 1026 and 1028).

In lines 1034 to 1038, the largest element, L(B), is exchanged with the last element, L(N). In line 1042, the list is shortened, and if more numbers remain to be sorted, line 1050 sends control back to 1022. The program executes from line 1022 again, but with a shorter sublist.

The output shown in Fig. 6.4 illustrates the fact that this program works for both positive and negative values. Furthermore, the original list may also contain duplicates. The ability to coalesce duplicates into one segment of a list will become very important in later applications.

Fred was quite satisfied with the selection sort until he tried it on two hundred elements. The senator's personal computer took forever to do the sorting. Then Fred discovered that the selection sort was a very slow-sort algorithm. The next day Fred began working on a faster method. The merge/sort is better to use when lists are very long.

Sorting by Merging

The basic idea in the merge/sort algorithm is successively to merge larger and larger sublists together until the entire list has been rearranged in order. The numerical example of Fig. 6.5 illustrates the process for N = 8 and a list in reverse order [Fig. 6.5(A)].

The merge/sort algorithm must start with sublists that are in order to begin with. This is provided in Fig. 6.5(B), where each pair of numbers has been exchanged to form ordered pairs. Thus, the list consists of four sublists when the merge steps begin. In Fig. 6.5(C), the pair (7, 8) is merged with the pair (5, 6) to form a larger sublist that is an ordered quadruple (5, 6, 7, 8). The next sublists are also merged into a quadruple consisting of (1, 2, 3, 4). In the final pass, shown in Fig. 6.5(D), the quads are merged into a single list containing N = 8 numbers in order.

The merge tree of Fig. 6.5(E) emphasizes the behavior of this method. Since there are no more than $(Log_2(N))$ passes in the merge

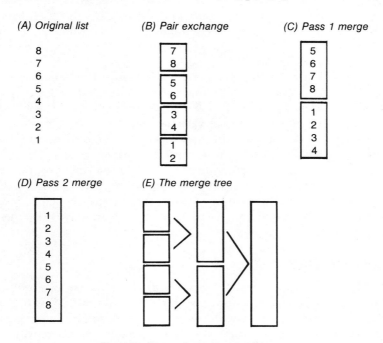

Fig. 6.5 Illustration of merge/sort

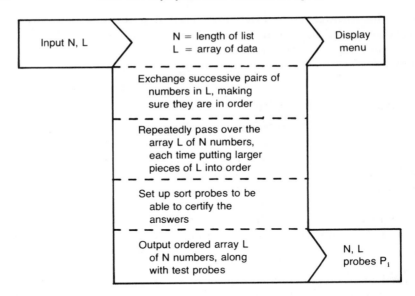

Fig. 6.6 BLUE$_0$ specification of merge/sort package

tree, we must provide up to (Log$_2$(N)) steps in the algorithm—one for each level of the tree. The BASIC functions LOG and INT will be needed to perform these calculations. In BASIC, the INT function computes the integer part of its argument. The LOG function computes the natural logarithm, so that we must divide by LOG(2) to obtain the correct logarithm value.

The blueprint of Fig. 6.6 outlines what must be done to program the merge/sort algorithm. The top-down refinement of BLUE$_0$ leads to modularization, as shown in Fig. 6.7. In Fig. 6.7(A), the DATA description section explains each variable and its function in the system.

In Fig. 6.7(E), we see the most complicated part of this system of modules. The merge module must be able to merge lists of any size and shape. For example, when N = 6, the merge operation must be able to merge two pairs into one quadruple, and a second single pair into a second quadruple. This merge requires checking the subscripts of each sublist to make sure they do not run off the end of the array.

The BASIC Routines

The blueprints of Fig. 6.7 are reduced to BASIC programs that will run on any personal computer with the features of BASIC displayed in Fig. 6.8. We can follow the development of these top-down, partially structured programs by understanding the pseudo-code blueprints first, and then reading the BASIC code secondly.

(A) BLUE₁ Specifications for Merge/Sort Package

1. PROGRAM: Merge/Sort

2. DATA:
    L1 = input array of numbers to be sorted, initially input
    L = temporary array for use in merge, initially unknown
    N = length of L and L_1, initially input
    P1 = sort probe to certify N, initially zero
    P2 = passes probe to certify correct number of passes made over the data; it should be equal to the value in this formula:
$$\text{Log}_2(N) - 1$$
      where the logarithm is rounded up to the nearest integer, initially zero
    P3 = exchange probe to certify correctness of the pair-exchange operations; it should be
$$N \qquad \text{if N is odd}$$
$$(N-1) \text{ if N is even}$$
      where N = length of list, initially zero
    P4 = merge probe to certify correctness of merging operation; it should be N when program stops, initially zero
    P5 = copy probe to certify correctness of copies from temporary list L_1 to L; it is computed as a check sum, initially zero
    P6 = input probe to certify P_5; it is computed as a check sum, initially zero

3. STEPS:
    3.1 Input N and L
        Display values
        Compute check sum, P6
    3.2 Set P1 probe to N
    3.3 Invoke the multiple pass routine
        Call PASSES
    3.4 Output sorted array and probes

(B) BLUE₁ Specification of the Pass Routine

1. PROGRAM: Passes

2. DATA:
    S1 = beginning of sublist to be ordered during the pass, initially one
    S2 = end of the sublist to be ordered during the pass, initially unknown
    S3 = number of passes required, computed from the formula:

$$\text{Log}_2(N)$$

    where this is done using the BASIC functions, INTeger and Natural LOGarithm:

$$\text{INT(LOG(N)/LOG(2))}$$

        initially computed
    L = length of sublist to be sorted, initially one

3. STEPS:
    3.1 Exchange pairs
        Call EXCHANGE routine

Fig. 6.7 Modularization of BLUE₀ specification

3.2 Compute number of passes, S3
3.3 Set up length, L2
3.4 Repeat loop S3 times
    3.4.1 Compute lengths and start and stop values of sublists
    3.4.2 Merge sublists to L1
         Call MERGE routine
    3.4.3 Repeatedly merge until all elements are done
    3.4.4 Copy from L1 to L
    3.4.5 Compute pass probe
3.5 Return

(C) BLUE₁ Specification of Merge Operation

1. PROGRAM: Merge

2. DATA:
    $I1$ = subscript of sublist one element, initially $S1$
    $I2$ = subscript of sublist two element, initially $S2$
    M = subscript of last element to be merged, initially computed
    $L2$ = length of sublists, initially given

3. STEPS:
    3.1 Set up starting values
        $I1 = S1$, $I1 = S2$, $M = S2 + L2 - 1$ or N, whichever is smaller.
    3.2 Repeat from start S1 to finish M
        If $I1 = S2$, then skip to "small"
        If $I2 = (M+1)$, then skip to "large"
        If $L(I1) = L(I2)$, then skip to "large"
        "small": Copy $L1(K) = L(I2)$
               Increment $I2 = I2+1$
               Skip to "end"
        "large": Copy $1(K) = L(I1)$
               Increment $I1 = I1 + 1$
        "end": Compute probe
    3.3 Return

(D) BLUE₁ Specification of Exchange Routine

1. PROGRAM: Exchange Pairs

2. DATA:
    T = temporary location, initially unknown

3. STEPS:
    3.1 Repeat in two's, until reaching N or $(N-1)$
        (that is, FOR J=1 TO N in steps of 2)
        3.1.1 If J=N, then skip to "end" (3.1.4)
        3.1.2 If $L(J) < L(J+1)$, then skip to "end" (3.1.4)
        3.1.3 Swap $L(J)$ and $L(J+1)$
        3.1.4 "end": Compute exchange probe
    3.2 RETURN

(E) BLUE₁ Specification of Copy Routine

1. PROGRAM: COPY L1 to L

Fig. 6.7 Continued

2. DATA:
   Same as Merge/Sort package

3. STEPS:
   3.1 Repeat N times (K=1, 2, ... N)
       L(K) = L1(K)
   3.2 Compute copy probe
   3.3 Return

Fig. 6.7 Continued

Line 1005 reserves 25 spaces each for the data array L and temporary array L1. The initialization steps of 1007 show how some dialects of BASIC allow multiple statements on a single line. The input statements are prompted by operator lead-through that is directed to device #D. The value of D determines where the prompt appears. When D = 0, the conversation is between keyboard and CRT. When D = 4, the response is printed on the local character printer. This feature allows the programmer to use a CRT while debugging the programs and then simply by adding

$$999 \quad \text{LET } D = 4$$

the output is diverted to the printer. Be sure to check the BASIC manual of each personal computer to see how I/O devices are selected, corresponding to the way we have shown device numbers here.

In line 1023, the check sum for L is stored in probe P6. Note in line 1045 that this is deducted from P5 to obtain zero when the correct check sum is obtained from the sorted array.

The PASSES routine beginning in location 2000 performs a pair-wise minor sort of the data. The pairs are then merged into longer and longer sublists until the full list has been ordered from the smallest to the largest value. In line 2043, the merge process is stopped when the sublist has been merged before the maximum number of values has been reached. This occurs whenever a sublist has a length *not* equal to a power of two.

The EXCHANGE routine is straightforward. Pairing the values in an odd-numbered list results in the last "pair" becoming a "singleton." This condition is checked in line 3020 of the subprogram.

The MERGE subprogram starting in line 4000 is a bit tricky. Remember that S1 and S2 point to the beginning of sublists to be merged. The subscripts I1 and I2 are used to "scan" the S1 and S2 sublists, respectively. Either I1 is increased (line 4042) or I2 is increased (line 4032), depending upon the value merged in order. The probe in line 4050 provides a weak guarantee that this routine is executed properly.

```
 999 LET D=4
1000 REM ****************************************************************
1001 REM                     MERGE/SORT PACKAGE
1002 REM                       COPYRIGHT 1977
1003 REM ****************************************************************
1004 REM
1005 DIM L[25],L1[25]
1006 REM   INITIALIZE PROBES
1007 LET P1=0; LET P2=0; LET P3=0; LET P4=0; LET P5=0; LET P6=0
1008 REM
1010 REM        INPUT N,L(.)
1012 PRINT#D, "MERGE/SORT ROUTINE."
1014 PRINT "INPUT LENGTH OF LIST : "; INPUT N
1016 PRINT "INPUT DISORDERED LIST......"
1018 FOR I=1 TO N
1020 PRINT#D, "DATA :", I, " = ";
1021 INPUT L[I]
1022 PRINT#D, L[I]
1023 LET P6=P6+L[I]
1025 NEXT I
1028 REM
1029 REM SORT PROBE 1
1030 LET P1=N
1032 REM
1034 REM CALL "PASSES"
1036 GOSUB 2000
1038 REM
1039 REM OUTPUT
1040 PRINT#D, "N = ", N, "PROBES......"
1041 PRINT#D, "PROBE 1 SHOULD BE ", N, " IS ", P1
1042 PRINT#D, "PROBE 2 SHOULD BE ", INT(LOG(N)/LOG(2)), " IS ", P2
1043 PRINT#D, "PROBE 3 SHOULD BE ", INT((N-1)/2)*2+1, " IS ", P3
1044 PRINT#D, "PROBE 4 SHOULD BE ", N, " IS ", P4
1045 PRINT#D, "PROBE 5 SHOULD BE 0.0, IS ", P5-P6
1050 FOR I=1 TO N
1052 PRINT#D, I, " : ", L[I]
1058 NEXT I
1060 PRINT#D, "END OF MERGE/SORT"
1070 STOP
```

(A)

```
2000 REM ****************************************************************
2001 REM                         PASSES
2002 REM ****************************************************************
2003 REM
2004 REM       EXCHANGE PAIRS
2010 GOSUB 3000
2012 REM
2014 REM       INITIALIZE PASSES, LENGTH, START SUBSCRIPT
2016 LET S3=INT(LOG(N)/LOG(2))
2018 LET L2=1
2019 REM
2020 REM       REPEAT PASSES S3 TIMES
2022 FOR I=1 TO S3
2024 LET L2=2*L2; LET S1=1
2025 REM    AGAIN
2026 LET S2=S1+L2
2029 REM
2030 REM       MERGE SUBLISTS
2032 GOSUB 4000
2034 REM
2040 REM       READY FOR NEXT PASS
2042 LET S1=S2+L2
2043 IF S1<=N THEN 2026
2044 REM    COPY L1 INTO L
2045 GOSUB 5000
2046 REM
2047 LET P2=I
2048 NEXT I
2049 REM
2050 RETURN
```

(B)

```
3000 REM     !*********************************************************
3001 REM                          EXCHANGE PAIRS
3002 REM     *********************************************************
3003 REM
3006 REM REPEAT
3010 FOR J=1 TO N STEP 2
3020 IF J=N THEN 3050
3030 IF L[J]<L[J+1] THEN 3050
3040 REM SWAP PAIRS
3042 LET T=L[J]; LET L[J]=L[J+1]; LET L[J+1]=T
3046 REM
3048 REM COMPUTE PROBE
3050 LET P3=J
3052 NEXT J
3054 RETURN
```

(C)

```
4000 REM     ***********************************************************
4001 REM                          MERGE SUBLISTS
4002 REM     ***********************************************************
4003 REM
4010 REM  -  INITIALIZE.
4011 LET I1=S1; LET I2=S2; LET M=S2+L2-1
4012 IF M<=N THEN 4022
4013 LET M=N
4014 REM
4020 REM     REPEAT
4022 FOR K=S1 TO M
4024 IF I1>=S2 THEN 4030
4026 IF I2>=(M+1) THEN 4040
4028 IF L[I1]<=L[I2] THEN 4040
4029 REM     SMALL
4030 LET L1[K]=L[I2]
4032 LET I2=I2+1
4034 GOTO 4050
4036 REM
4038 REM     LARGE
4040 LET L1[K]=L[I1]
4042 LET I1=I1+1
4044 REM
4046 REM     END
4050 LET P4=K
4055 NEXT K
4060 RETURN
```

(D)

```
5000 REM     ***********************************************************
5001 REM                          COPY L1 INTO L
5002 REM     ***********************************************************
5003 REM
5004 LET P5=0
5005 REM        REPEAT LOOP
5010 FOR K=1 TO N
5015 LET L[K]=L1[K]
5017 LET P5=P5+L[K]
5019 NEXT K
5020 REM
5030 RETURN
```

(E)

Fig. 6.8 (A) Main program for merge/sort package, (B) subprogram passes for merge/sort package, (C) exchange subprogram for merge/sort package, (D) merge subprogram for merge/sort package, and (E) copy subprogram for merge/sort package

Finally, COPY in lines 5000 to 5030 sums the values after each merge and moves them from the temporary array L1 back into array L. P5 is used as a check sum probe.

Test Case

Figure 6.9 illustrates the execution of the programs in Fig. 6.8. The device number, #D, is set to the printer:

$$999 \quad \text{LET D} = 4$$

This forces all printing to the character printer rather than the CRT.

The sample data of Fig. 6.9 shows ten zip codes. The program is certified as correct because all probes are as they should be. The sorted zip codes are finally printed in order.

The zip codes printed in Fig. 6.9 display an important feature of sorting. The duplicate values numbers like 97321, 97355, and 97401 cluster together when sorted. This feature will be essential in a later chapter.

Bigger Is Worser

Fred Byte leaned back in his chair before Senator Gambit's personal computer and relaxed when he obtained the results of Fig. 6.9. The merge/sort package was going to work just fine, he thought. Only one problem remained.

The senator's mailing list consisted of thousands of names and addresses instead of only 25 as allowed by the BASIC programs of Fig. 6.8. Fred thought about this as he sipped his drink.

The first idea that came to Fred's mind was to increase the size of the arrays in BASIC. Instead of limiting the mailing list to 25, Fred could make them 2500 values long. To do so would require over 5000 words of main memory, and the senator's personal computer was a 16KB memory system. Of this 16KB, only 4KB remains after loading the operating system and BASIC interpreter.

Fred's frown furrowed his forehead as he contemplated future frustrations. In order to store larger lists of zip-coded data, he would have to turn to the *file.*

File Structures

Fred spent the next few days learning about the file-handling characteristics of his personal computer. Actually, every system has the file structures discussed in the previous chapter. The differences in file I/O from one system to another will be revealed by different

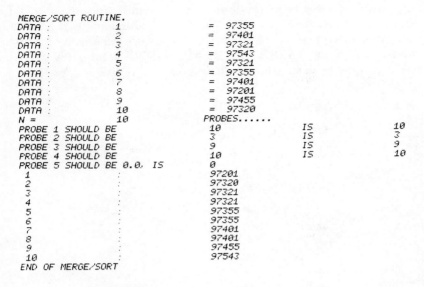

```
MERGE/SORT ROUTINE.
DATA :        1        =   97355
DATA :        2        =   97401
DATA :        3        =   97321
DATA :        4        =   97543
DATA :        5        =   97321
DATA :        6        =   97355
DATA :        7        =   97401
DATA :        8        =   97201
DATA :        9        =   97455
DATA :       10        =   97320
N =          10           PROBES......
PROBE 1 SHOULD BE         10         IS        10
PROBE 2 SHOULD BE          3         IS         3
PROBE 3 SHOULD BE          9         IS         9
PROBE 4 SHOULD BE         10         IS        10
PROBE 5 SHOULD BE 0.0, IS  0
 1          :            97201
 2          :            97320
 3          :            97321
 4          :            97321
 5          :            97355
 6          :            97355
 7          :            97401
 8          :            97401
 9          :            97455
10          :            97543
END OF MERGE/SORT
```

Fig. 6.9   Sample run of merge/sort package

dialects of BASIC. Fred had to determine which statements in his version of BASIC were the proper ones to do file I/O.

Fred's BASIC allowed two types of file structures: (1) sequential, and (2) random. In order to implement an indexed file structure, Fred would have to construct his own subfiles and write programs to manipulate the data stored in file records. The BASIC commands useful for manipulation of files are summarized in Fig. 6.10. Note that the

	Used in This Book	Other Versions
(1) Sequential	OPEN #	OPEN #
	END #	CLOSE #
	EOF #	
	PRINT #	WRITE #
	INPUT #	READ #
(2) Random	OPEN #	OPEN #
	END #	CLOSE #
	PRINT #	WRITE #
	INPUT #	READ #
	RESTORE #	RESTORE #

Fig. 6.10   File commands in BASIC

only difference between random file commands and sequential file commands is the addition of a RESTORE statement to the random file commands. Also notice the trivial departure of one BASIC from another. In some BASICs, the READ/WRITE commands are used solely to transfer data from the main memory to disk or tape.

```
105 DIM E$[8], M$[15], R$[18], B$[15]
110 PRINT "STORE A SEQUENTIAL FILE IN DEVICE D"
120 PRINT "ENTER FILE NAME : "; INPUT E$
130 PRINT "ENTER DEVICE NUMBER (1 OR 2) : "; INPUT D
140 REM
145 REM      OPEN FILE D
150 REM
155 OPEN#D, E$
170 REM
175 PRINT "NAME : "; INPUT M$
176 PRINT "STREET : "; INPUT R$
177 PRINT "CITY & STATE : "; INPUT B$
178 PRINT "ZIP : "; INPUT Z
180 PRINT#D, Z; M$; R$; B$
185 PRINT "ENTER 0 IF DONE : "; INPUT Z
190 IF Z=0 THEN 199
195 GOTO 170
196 REM
197 REM      CLOSE FILE D
198 REM
199 END#D
200 RETURN
```

(A)

```
5 DIM F$[8], N$[15], S$[18], C$[15]
10 PRINT "LIST A SEQUENTIAL FILE FROM DEVICE D"
20 PRINT "ENTER FILE NAME : "; INPUT F$
30 PRINT "ENTER DEVICE NUMBER (1 OR 2) : "; INPUT D
40 REM
45 REM      OPEN FILE D
50 REM
55 OPEN#D, F$
60 PRINT "ENTER 0 FOR CRT, 4 FOR PRINTER DISPLAY : "; INPUT D1
65 PRINT#D1, "FILE : ", F$, " FROM DEVICE : ", D, " LISTING"
67 PRINT#D1, "_____"
68 PRINT#D1
70 REM
75 INPUT#D, Z; N$; S$; C$
80 IF EOF#D THEN 99
85 PRINT#D1, TAB(10), N$
86 PRINT#D1, TAB(10), S$
87 PRINT#D1, TAB(10), C$
88 PRINT#D1, TAB(10), Z
89 PRINT#D1, "_____"
90 REM
95 GOTO 70
96 REM
97 REM      CLOSE FILE D
98 REM
99 END#D
100 RETURN
```

(B)

Fig. 6.11 (A) The PUT subprogram for writing a sequential file, and (B) the GET subprogram for reading a sequential file

Figure 6.11 demonstrates use of these commands in two programs: (1) PUT stores data in a sequential file called F$, whereas (2) GET retrieves data from the sequential file. We can learn a few lessons about file structure by studying these examples.

In the PUT routine of Fig. 6.11(A), we perform all three basic steps in storing data into a sequential file. First, the file is opened (see line 155). The device #D is opened for a file named E$. For example, D is read as 2, and E$ is read as "MAILERS." The values of M$, R$, B$, and Z are obtained through statements 175 to 178. Then in line 180, these values are written to the sequential file number, #D. Note the use of semicolons between fields in the record:

$$Z; M\$; R\$; B\$$$

The semicolon causes each record to be packed into consecutive locations of the file device. If a colon had been used, the variables in the record would be spaced apart as if they were printed on a printer. This approach would use more space than needed.

The final step in the PUT program closes the file (see line 199) and causes a file marker called an EOF (end-of-file) mark to be written. The EOF is used to signal when an end of file has been reached when the records are read from the file. We see how this is done in Fig. 6.11(B)—line 80.

The output from the GET routine is shown in Fig. 6.1(A). It was obtained running the programs from GOSUBs:

```
210   GOSUB   5
220   GOSUB 105
225   STOP
```

The RESTORE statement was not needed to write the GET and PUT subprograms because of the use of sequential instead of random files. The fundamental limitation of tape prevents rapid GET and PUT execution in any mode of operation other than sequential. We must use a disk device before the RESTORE command is useful in BASIC.

Device Considerations

Fred Byte began working out a design that would apply file I/O techniques to the mailing list problem. He began by converting the merge/sort program to a file structure system in place of the array structure.

His idea was to replace the L and L1 arrays of Fig. 6.8 with an index subfile, as illustrated in the output of Fig. 6.1(B). That is, each zip code is stored in a record of index L along with the value of a record number corresponding with the records shown in Fig.

Random index subfile, "L"   Random master file, "mailer"

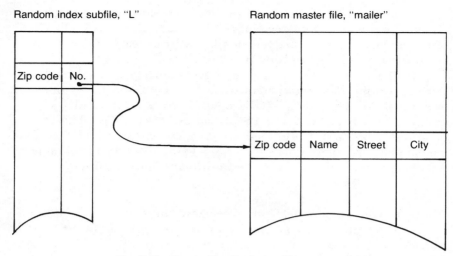

Fig. 6.12   The mailing list index file structure

6.1(a). Thus, zip code 96101 is stored with record number 3. This approach gives Fred the index file structure shown in Fig. 6.12.

The file structure that Fred designed in Fig. 6.12 can be sorted using the merge/sort programs if Fred converts the array data structure to a file structure that manipulates the random index subfile, "L." Since each record in "L" contains a record number pointing to the corresponding master file record, Fred can sort the index "L" and then produce an ordered output by random accessing the master records in their proper order.

The index "L" is often called a *sort train* in data processing. This method of sorting a file through an auxiliary index file is also called *tag sorting*. It is a very common technique used in big systems but requires random access devices.

A personal computer must be provided with a random access storage device in order to perform the tag sort described above. The three devices that meet these requirements are: (1) mini floppies, (2) floppies, or (3) cartridge disks. We will consider the physical organization of the first two only, since the last device is very expensive.

A mini floppy is organized in exactly the same way as a floppy diskette. The difference is in retrieval speed and storage capacity. For example, the mini floppy will generally provide storage for several 100,000 characters, whereas a floppy will generally provide for storage of up to a million characters of data.

Both devices are organized into 256-byte physical records called *sectors*. A sector is the basic unit of storage addressed by the BASIC RESTORE command; consequently, we see that the first device consideration is the Wasted Space Rule.

Wasted space rule: A diskette is randomly accessed in units called a *sector*. If the logical record is larger than a sector, it must be divided into smaller parts; if the logical record is smaller than a sector, then random access is to a sector rather than a logical record. Each record will occupy an entire 256-byte sector.

The advantage of random access outweighs the disadvantages of the Wasted Space Rule. We could, of course, reformat each packed sector into one record per sector before sorting and then pack the records into fewer sectors after the random access sort has been accomplished. This technique is, in fact, often used.

A floppy contains 1K sectors, whereas a mini floppy contains 360 sectors (as technology improves floppy manufacturing, this density increases). Otherwise, the only consideration is one of cost and demand for storage space.

A sequential READ/WRITE in BASIC produces packed records on diskette. A random READ/WRITE using the RESTORE command produces *one record per sector* (unpacked) on diskette.

It became obvious to Fred Byte that the senator had chosen tape when he should have chosen diskette for his personal computer. Thus, the next day Fred and the senator returned to the computer shop to buy a diskette subsystem.

Necessity Is the Mother of Technique

Fred realized the necessity of random access. His modifications to the merge/sort package are shown in Fig. 6.13. This program was used to produce the results of Fig. 6.1.

The additions to merge/sort were made according to the following rules:

1. DIM arrays L and L1 are replaced by files L and L1, along with OPEN and END statements.
2. Every reference to L and L1 is replaced by a random access file I/O routine.
3. Every random access I/O is a PRINT/INPUT command preceded by a RESTORE command.

These rules were applied to the merge/sort package of Fig. 6.8 by disturbing the programs as little as possible. In general, you should write a GET and PUT routine and use a GOSUB to execute them. In Fig. 6.13, we have chosen to modify the affected segments of code rather than add routines because of the simplicity it offers and to demonstrate the idea with a previously studied program.

Lines 900 to 922 merely open the two files that replace arrays L and L1. In lines 1046 and 1047, these files are closed, and then file "L" is opened for output in line 1048.

```
900 REM    MODIFIED MERGE/SORT PACKAGE
901 REM
902 REM         OPEN FILES L AND L1
910 OPEN#1, "L"
920 OPEN#2, "L1"
922 PRINT "SELECT OUTPUT DEVICE (0=CRT, 4=PRINTER) : "; INPUT D
1000 REM *********************************************************
1001 REM                  FILE MERGE/SORT PACKAGE
1002 REM                       COPYRIGHT 1977
1003 REM *********************************************************
1004 REM
1005 REM NO ARRAY NEEDED
1006 REM   INITIALIZE PROBES
1007 LET P1=0; LET P2=0; LET P3=0; LET P4=0; LET P5=0; LET P6=0
1008 REM
1010 REM         INPUT N, L(.)
1012 PRINT#D, "MERGE/SORT ROUTINE."
1014 PRINT "INPUT LENGTH OF LIST : "; INPUT N
1016 PRINT "INPUT DISORDERED LIST......"
1017 FOR I=1 TO N
1018 REM       RANDOM FILE ACCESS
1019 RESTORE#1, I-1
1020 PRINT#D, "DATA : ", I, " = ";
1021 INPUT L
1022 PRINT#D, L
1023 LET P6=P6+L
1024 PRINT#1, L; I
1025 REM      RANDOM WRITE DONE
1026 NEXT I
1028 REM
1029 REM SORT PROBE 1
1030 LET P1=N
1032 REM
1034 REM CALL "PASSES"
1036 GOSUB 2000
1038 REM
1039 REM OUTPUT
1040 PRINT#D, "N = ", N, "PROBES......"
1041 PRINT#D, "PROBE 1 SHOULD BE ", N, " IS ", P1
1042 PRINT#D, "PROBE 2 SHOULD BE ", INT(LOG(N)/LOG(2)), " IS ", P2
1043 PRINT#D, "PROBE 3 SHOULD BE ", INT((N-1)/2)*2+1, " IS ", P3
1044 PRINT#D, "PROBE 4 SHOULD BE ", N, " IS ", P4
1045 PRINT#D, "PROBE 5 SHOULD BE 0.0, IS ", P5-P6
1046 END#1
1047 END#2
1048 OPEN#1, "L"
1049 REM
1050 FOR I=1 TO N
1051 REM     RANDOM FILE READ
1052 RESTORE#1, I-1
1053 INPUT#1, L; J
1055 PRINT#D, I, " : ", L, J
1058 NEXT I
1060 PRINT#D, "END OF MERGE/SORT"
1065 END#1
1070 STOP
2000 REM *********************************************************
2001 REM                        PASSES
2002 REM *********************************************************
2003 REM
2004 REM       EXCHANGE PAIRS
2010 GOSUB 3000
2012 REM
2014 REM       INITIALIZE PASSES, LENGTH, START SUBSCRIPT
2016 LET S3=INT(LOG(N)/LOG(2))
2018 LET L2=1
2019 REM
2020 REM       REPEAT PASSES S3 TIMES
2022 FOR I=1 TO S3
2024 LET L2=2*L2; LET S1=1
2025 REM   AGAIN
```

```
2026 LET S2=S1+L2
2029 REM
2030 REM       MERGE SUBLISTS
2032 GOSUB 4000
2034 REM
2040 REM        READY FOR NEXT PASS
2042 LET S1=S2+L2
2043 IF S1<=N THEN 2026
2044 REM    COPY L1 INTO L
2045 GOSUB 5000
2046 REM
2047 LET P2=I
2048 NEXT I
2049 REM
2050 RETURN
3000 REM *****************************************************************
3001 REM                        EXCHANGE PAIRS
3002 REM *****************************************************************
3003 REM
3006 REM REPEAT
3010 FOR J=1 TO N STEP 2
3015 IF J=N THEN 3050
3018 REM       RANDOM ACCESS FILES
3020 RESTORE#1, J-1
3021 INPUT#1, L; W
3022 RESTORE#1, J
3023 INPUT#1, L9; W9
3030 IF L<L9 THEN 3050
3031 REM
3040 REM SWAP PAIRS
3042 RESTORE#1, J-1
3043 PRINT#1, L9; W9
3044 RESTORE#1, J
3045 PRINT#1, L; W
3046 REM
3048 REM COMPUTE PROBE
3050 LET P3=J
3052 NEXT J
3054 RETURN
4000 REM *****************************************************************
4001 REM                        MERGE SUBLISTS
4002 REM *****************************************************************
4003 REM
4010 REM       INITIALIZE.
4011 LET I1=S1; LET I2=S2; LET M=S2+L2-1
4012 IF M<=N THEN 4022
4013 LET M=N
4014 REM
4020 REM       REPEAT
4022 FOR K=S1 TO M
4023 IF I1>=S2 THEN 4030
4024 RESTORE#1, I1-1
4025 INPUT#1, L; W
4026 IF I2>=(M+1) THEN 4040
4027 RESTORE#1, I2-1
4028 INPUT#1, L9; W9
4029 IF L<=L9 THEN 4040
4030 RESTORE#2, K-1
4031 PRINT#2, L9; W9
4034 LET I2=I2+1
4035 GOTO 4050
4040 RESTORE#2, K-1
4041 PRINT#2, L; W
4042 LET I1=I1+1
4044 REM
```

Fig. 6.13   Random index file merge/sort package

```
4046 REM      END
4050 LET P4=K
4055 NEXT K
4060 RETURN
5000 REM  ***********************************************************
5001 REM                          COPY L1 INTO L
5002 REM  ***********************************************************
5003 REM
5004 LET P5=0
5009 REM      REPEAT COPY
5010 FOR K=1 TO N
5011 RESTORE#2,K-1
5012 INPUT#2,L1;W
5013 RESTORE#1,K-1
5014 PRINT#1,L1;W
5017 LET P5=P5+L1
5019 NEXT K
5020 REM
5030 RETURN
```

Fig. 6.13 Continued

The RESTORE #1 command used in lines 1019 and 1052 demonstrates how to place RESTORE immediately before a PRINT or INPUT statement in order to force a random WRITE or READ. Observe the record number (I − 1) used in these RESTORE statements. The record numbers of a file begin at zero and run to (n − 1), whereas an array subscript runs from one to (n). Beware of this pitfall.

The pairwise exchange of records illustrated in lines 3021 through 3023 demonstrates once again the importance of the RESTORE command. In this segment of code, variables L9 and W9 are temporary variables used to compare each number in the pair. The W and W9 pointers are copied along with their corresponding zip codes (L, L9) to keep track of the records in the master file (not included in this program). The actual exchange takes place in lines 3042 to 3045.

The random access invention forces major changes in the way the merge subprogram operates. Lines 4024 to 4041 show this. In each case of an access to diskette, the RESTORE command is used to position to the proper record (sector).

Finally, the copy routine of lines 5000 to 5030 restores "L" from file "L1." In the copy position, we have used L1 as an input and print variable, but, of course, L9 would have worked as well.

Fred Byte and Senator Gambit managed to mail 50,000 pamphlets to registered voters. The senator got elected, Fred learned a lot about file I/O and personal computers, and Catfish Dave married a young volunteer and lives in the Cascade Mountains. The last words spoken to both Fred and the senator by Catfish were, "Reckon I done what I could for the world. The rest is up to politicians and whippersnappers like Freddie and that gol dern computer."

Catfish disappeared down the road with his bride, and Fred returned to his personal computer projects. "Bert, I got this idea. . . ."

Chapter Seven

Dr. Goode's Accounts Receivable

"I was surprised to read about dad's system in the Sunday paper. At the time we started working on the clinic's personal computer, I thought it was a lot of fun. Everyone played the game that was delivered with the system, and then the hard work began. Now that I think back about it, I recall those days as being exciting. It was an adventure. A lot of improvements have been made since, but the basic program that I wrote then is still working away inside the computer."

Jacob Elan Goode, 1977

In Chap. 2, we analyzed Dr. Goode's clinic and designed a system for alleviating the billing load. The idea behind the medical accounts receivable system is the same as the idea behind any accounts receivable system. The details of a medical system may differ slightly, but the philosophy remains the same.

Accounts receivable systems are typically one of three kinds, as follows:

1. Balance-only systems
2. Balance-forward systems
3. Open-item systems

In a balance-only system, the amount of information stored from one month to the next is minimized to keep storage requirements and system complexity to a minimum. In addition to the patient's name, address, telephone number, and insurance company, we keep only an outstanding balance due. At the end of each month, this balance is added to new charges (called the transaction amount) or payments, and a statement requesting payment of the remaining balance is sent to the patient. In a balance-only system, the current balance and updates used to adjust the previous balance are the only information provided by the statement.

In a balance-forward A/R system, the patient receives added detail concerning charges. Each statement contains a list of charges made

109

during the billing period. The list of charges are transactions posted against the previous balance and give the patient an idea of what he was charged for each item.

The balance-forward system does not provide detail about the previous balance or how it was derived. If the patient fails to remember how the previous balance was derived, there is no way to find this out from the statement. The balance-forward system represents a compromise between storage requirements and detail.

The open-item A/R system provides the greatest amount of detail for the customer or patient. Each transaction during the life of an outstanding bill is listed on the statement. A patient may object to one or more of the items and return a payment for only part of the bill. The unpaid items are then listed on the subsequent bill along with new transaction items. Each item that has not been paid for is carried forward to the next billing period. This system gives patients a detailed outline of charges no matter when they were made against their account.

Dr. Goode selected the balance-forward A/R method. In the remainder of this chapter, we will develop balance-forward system programs for a minimal A/R system that can be expanded into a system for almost any business, home, or office.

The Clinic Superbill

Dr. Goode's biggest worry is insurance billing. The insurance companies require detailed information about each patient and details about each transaction. As a result, the clinic is required to fill out dozens of insurance forms each time a patient comes in.

The first step in relieving the clinic's A/R burden was to simplify insurance billing. This is exactly the function of the superbill. A superbill is a single sheet of paper used by each physician to record the illness and treatment rendered a patient. An example of a miniature superbill is shown in Fig. 7.1.

The superbill contains all the information required by the insurance companies and all the information needed to generate billing statements to patients. The insurance company, for instance, requires the use of medical code (CPT) numbers. The CPT numbers are recorded next to each illness and each treatment. A check-up is CPT code 10001, whereas the treatment indicated in Fig. 7.1 is CPT code 501. These numbers are used by the insurance company computer.

The superbill also contains enough information to generate a statement. In Fig. 7.1, we have illustrated a two-transaction superbill requiring two charges. These charges are entered into the personal computer as transactions. They are posted against a master file containing

PATIENT ID _____

NAME _____ DATE _____

ADDRESS _____ CITY _____ ZIP _____

TELEPHONE _____

ILLNESS (DIAGNOSIS)

Virus	90001		Check-up	10001	✓
Measles	80010		Lockjaw	40001	
Mumps	80020		Mono	40005	
Appendicitis	90100		Diabetes	60100	
Strep throat	80030		Hepatitis	60200	
Skin rash	70120		Pox	40100	

TREATMENT

Urine test	501	✓	Surgery	400	
Drugs	550		Anesthetics	410	
Emerg. room	950		Outpatient	420	
Pills	100		Inoculation	510	

Fig. 7.1 A mini superbill for Dr. Goode

the patient's name, address, telephone number, and previous balance. Once posted, the statement is printed for mailing.

Building a Master File

The information contained at the top of a superbill will already be known to the clinic for all regular patients. This information is kept on ledger cards in most manual A/R systems. In a computer-based A/R system, ledger cards are replaced by a mass storage file called the MASTER file.

The MASTER file is sorted into order by a unique number called the *patient ID*. Each billable patient is assigned a number when visiting the clinic for the first time. This is shown by the MASTER file listing in Fig. 7.2.

The master file contains records consisting of patient ID, name, date of entry, address, telephone number, and current balance due.

```
 1000        :      G. K. BARNES      10/01/77
             4895 MEEKER
             ALBANY, OR.
              97321      503-928-4086    $            35
 ----------------------------------------------------------
 1001        :      T. G. LEWIS       10/01/77
             57 E. ISABELLA
             LEBANON, OR.
              97355      503-258-4195    $            10
 ----------------------------------------------------------
 1010        :       B. JOHNSON       10/01/77
             1412 SALEM RD.
             ALBANY, OR.
              97321      503-928-5980    $             0
 ----------------------------------------------------------
 2000        :      CRAK. JONES       10/01/77
             P. O. BOX 10
             SWEETWATER, OR.
              97400      503-555-1212    $             0
 ----------------------------------------------------------
 2005        :      CATFISH DAVE      10/01/77
             451 SW. OAK
             SWEETWATER, OR.
              97400      503-555-1212    $            25
 ----------------------------------------------------------
 1            0                 70                  5
```

Fig. 7.2 The master file listing generated by the master file creation program in Dr. Goode's clinic

In Fig. 7.2, the master file contains five entries, each with a unique patient ID, and each with an initial balance due.

Also notice the check sum probe values printed on the last line of Fig. 7.2. These are correctness checks for the program, but they are also useful for the clinic. The first number indicates what number will be assigned to the next transaction entered against this file. The second number is the dollar amount of transactions currently remaining to be posted. The third number ($70) is the sum of balances outstanding in the file, and the final number is the total number of entries (patients) in the master file.

Each record of the master file is *signed* with a date. In Fig. 7.2, the date (10/01/77) refers to the file creation date. This date provides an audit trail for validating the file. Each time the balance of any record is altered, the audit trail date is updated to show when the change was made. This change and signing process will occur when the transactions are posted against the master file and also when statements are generated.

Building the Account Table

In many A/R systems, the superbill is stored in a file called the *account table* or *description file*. This file enables the clinic to set standard prices for each treatment and let the computer look up charges in the description table. Use of it avoids making inputs, and the operator does not have to remember or look for the charge amount.

We will not use an account table in the sample programs to follow. Instead, the description and dollar charge are entered for each transaction.

In order to implement the account table, we would write a program to enter the CPT code along with a description and dollar charge. This file is accessed randomly by CPT code key. Thus an index subfile may be retained to assist in the random access.

The index file may be sorted to speed look-up, but searching for the appropriate CPT code record is slow at best. The system is greatly degraded by the addition of a CPT look-up. What can be done?

A technique calling *hashing* is useful in a case like this. Indeed, we will find the notion of a *hashing function* unavoidable in an application in Chap. 9.

If the record number REMAINDER is empty, then the record is written into this position using a direct (random) access. We can do this in BASIC as follows:

```
400   LET Q = INT(K/N)
410   LET R = INT(K − N * Q)
415   RESTORE #F, R
420   INPUT #F, K1
430   IF K1 = 0 THEN 500
440   LET R = R + Q
450   IF R < N THEN 415
460   LET Q1 = INT(R/N)
470   LET R = INT(R − N * Q1)
480   GOTO 415
```

If the REMAINDER is not empty, as is the case in records 1, 2, 5, 11, and 15 of Fig. 7.3, then a subsequent probe into another record position is required. The subsequent probe is made in record position REMAINDER + QUOTIENT. This process is illustrated above in lines 440 through 480. Note that addition of $R + Q$ may produce a record number larger than N. In this case, we must produce a second, third, fourth, etc., remainder in order to keep the value of R between zero and $(N − 1)$.

A hashing function is a computer program that converts keys into record numbers. The keys are taken from each record and used to compute each record's location in the file.

For example, the account table of the superbill in Fig. 7.1 can be stored in a random file that is accessed by a hashing function. The hashing function performs the correspondence illustrated in Fig. 7.3. Records 0, 3, 6, 7, 16, 18, 20, 21, and 24 are left empty while the other records are directly accessed using the hashing function.

All we need to know to access 60100 directly, say, is the method of computing record number 12, given key 60100.

The *division* hashing function was used to insert the account table items into the file of length N = 29 (see Fig. 7.3). Here is how it works.

The remainder and quotient after division by N = 29 is obtained:

$$\text{Remainder of } (60100/29) = 12$$
$$\text{Quotient of } (60100/29) = 2072$$

In Fig. 7.3, the collisions that occur because a record already occupies a record position results in subsequent searches. For example, when record position 11 becomes occupied by CPT keyed record 420, it is necessary to search positions 14, 28, 13, 27, 12, and 26 before finding an empty record at position 11.

CPT Code Key	Record No. (Collision Record Nos.)
—	0
40005	1 (14)
950	2 (22, 25, 28)
—	3
420	4
510	5 (17)
—	6
—	7
501	8
80020	9
40001	10
420	11 (14, 28, 13, 27, 12, 26)
60100	12
100	13
90001	14
60200	15 (25, 12, 28)
—	16
550	17
—	18
80030	19
—	20
—	21
40100	22
400	23
—	24
10001	25
90100	26
70120	27
80010	28

Fig. 7.3 Account table file using hashing (N = 29).

The hashed file of Fig. 7.3 provides extremely rapid look-up. The worst case of file accesses in the account table occurs for 420 at record number 11. The best case occurs in many places with a single access.

To perform a look-up, we repeat the same search pattern. Thus, to get the record corresponding to CPT = 510, we compute R and Q, as follows:

$$R = \text{Remainder of } (510/29) = 17$$
$$Q = \text{Quotient of } (510/29) = 17$$

We try record number 17 but discover that CPT = 550 is stored there. Thus we add R + Q to obtain 34. Since 34 > 29, we produce a second remainder and try again.

$$R1 = \text{Remainder of } (34/29) = 5$$

The second attempt with R = 5 produces a match: 510 = 510. Thus, we were able to locate item 510 in two search probes.

Hashing functions are extremely useful and easy to implement in personal computers. We will return to the concept with a full example in this chapter, but in the example presented here we will not employ the technique. Indeed, we will not employ an account table, but it is a most appropriate method to use in this application.

The BASIC Routines

Figures 7.4, 7.5, and 7.6 provide the master file build subsystem for Dr. Goode's A/R system. In Fig. 7.4, the general approach is exposed. Files are opened and patient data are input and written to a random access file. An index file is also created to aid in merge/sorting (see Chap. 4).

The $BLUE_0$ specification also includes a check sum probe for error detection and produces a listing (see Fig. 7.2).

A transaction file header record is written before the master file build program halts. This header contains probe information and the starting record number for inputting transactions. This information is used by the transaction program and the posting program.

Figure 7.5 illustrates a refinement of Fig. 7.4. The master file is called "MASTER," and its index file is called "MINDEX." Each input record is stored in a string field or numeric field as it is read.

The BASIC routine of Fig. 7.6 provides a detailed specification of the file manipulation and control of input to "MASTER" and "MINDEX." The details of this program will be explained section by section.

The MASTER Account File Input Routine

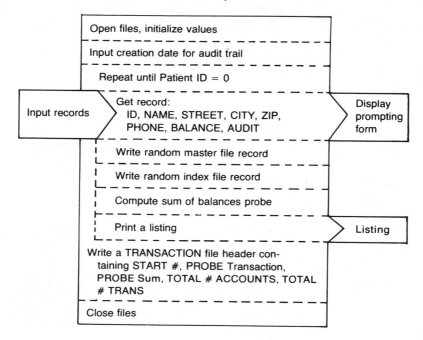

Fig. 7.4   BLUE₀ specification for accounts receivable master

5	Set D = printer, for hard copy output
20	Declare string variables
40–45	Open files
50	Get audit trail date
60–79	Input records until ID = 0
70–89	Store randomly. The field separators "P" and "B" are used to separate strings with digits from numbers with digits. This prevents a mixup when reading these fields back into main memory.
90	Sum total balance
100–115	Print listing and update count
125–127	Close files
130–140	Open transaction file called "TRANS" and write a header. Close "TRANS."

---

1. PROGRAM: Input Master File Records

2. DATA:
    I   = patient identification number, initially input
    N$ = patient last (family) name, initially input
    S$ = street address of patient, initially input
    C$ = city and state, initially input
    Z   = Zip code, initially input
    P$ = phone number, initially input
    B   = outstanding balance due, initially input
    A$ = audit trail date, initially input
    P1 = check sum of balances, initially zero
    P2 = check sum of transactions, initially zero
    S1 = beginning record number of transaction file, initially 1
    T1 = total number of master file records, initially 0

3. STEPS:
    3.1. Open file #1 as "MASTER"
            file #2 as "MINDEX"
            initialize P1, P2, S1, T1
    3.2. Input date of file creation, A$
    3.3. Input MASTER file records until I=0:
            3.3.1. Input I, N$, S$, C$, Z, P$, B
            3.3.2. Write #1; I, N$, S$, C$, Z, P$, B, A$ (random)
            3.3.3. Write #2; I, record number (random)
            3.3.4. Calculate P1 sum of B
            3.3.5. Print listing: I, N$, S$, C$, Z, P$, B, A$
            3.3.6. Increment T1
    3.4. Close files #1 and #2
    3.5. Open #2 as "TRANS"
    3.6. Write transaction file header:
            S1 = 2, P2 = 0, P1, T1
    3.7. Close #2

Fig. 7.5 $BLUE_1$ specification for accounts receivable

This program was run to produce the output shown in Fig. 7.2. We will use the sample master file of this figure to illustrate a statement generation program in the next section.

The First Solution: Back to Sorting

The transaction file contains payments and charges as they are collected throughout the month. They are keyed on patient ID as before, but they contain an audit trail date of creation, description of treatment, and the amount billed. This information is printed on each statement when posted against the master file records. But how are the transactions combined into a single statement?

```
  5 LET D=4
 10 REM ******************************************************************
 11 REM                      A/R MASTER CREATE PROGRAM
 12 REM                         COPYRIGHT 1977
 13 REM ******************************************************************
 20 DIM N$[16], S$[16], C$[16], P$[12], A$[8]
 30 LET P1=0: LET P2=0: LET S1=1: LET T1=0
 38 REM ---------------------------------------------------------------
 40 OPEN#1, "MASTER"
 45 OPEN#2, "MINDEX"
 49 REM ---------------------------------------------------------------
 50 PRINT "DATE OF CREATION MM/DD/YY : "; INPUT A$
 55 REM ---------------------------------------------------------------
 60 PRINT "PATIENT ID                   : "; INPUT I
 61 IF I=0 THEN 125
 62 PRINT "NAME (MAXIMUM 16 LETTERS) :"; INPUT N$
 63 PRINT "STREET (MAX 16 CHARACTERS): "; INPUT S$
 64 PRINT "CITY & STATE (16 CHAR.)    "; INPUT C$
 65 PRINT "ZIP CODE                  : "; INPUT Z
 66 PRINT "PHONE (AREA-PRE-NUM)      : "; INPUT P$
 67 PRINT "STARTING BALANCE          $"; INPUT B
 69 REM ---------------------------------------------------------------
 70 RESTORE#1, T1
 75 PRINT#1, I, N$, S$, C$, Z, "P", P$, B, "B", A$
 80 RESTORE#2, T1
 85 PRINT#2, I, T1
 89 REM ---------------------------------------------------------------
 90 LET P1=P1+B
100 PRINT#D, I, TAB(10), "   ", N$, TAB(30), A$
101 PRINT#D, TAB(10), S$
102 PRINT#D, TAB(10), C$
103 PRINT#D, TAB(10), Z, TAB(20), P$, TAB(35), "$ ", B
104 PRINT#D, "---------------------------------------------------------
105 REM ---------------------------------------------------------------
110 LET T1=T1+1
115 REM ---------------------------------------------------------------
119 GOTO 60
125 END#1
127 END#2
129 REM ---------------------------------------------------------------
130 OPEN#2, "TRANS"
132 RESTORE#2
135 PRINT#2, S1, P2, P1, T1
137 PRINT#D, S1, P2, P1, T1
140 END#2
150 RETURN
```

Fig. 7.6   BLUE$_2$ specification for accounts receivable master program in BASIC

The Transaction File

The transaction file contains a scrambled list of charges. Patients may visit the clinic at random times throughout the month, and this produces a random list of transactions.

Of course, Dr. Goode could collect all of the superbills for a given patient into one pile and then enter them into the personal computer on the day posting is to be done. This solution requires work on the part of the clinic staff, and the personal computer was purchased to avoid such effort.

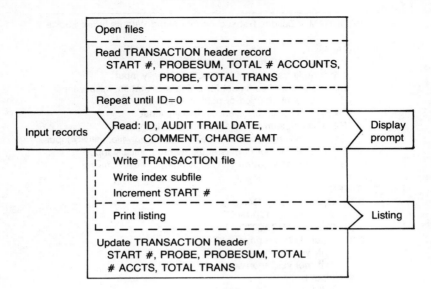

Fig. 7.7 BLUE$_0$ for the transaction file input routine

The obvious solution for Dr. Goode is to direct the personal computer to sort the transactions into ascending order before posting them. Recall that records with identical values are sorted into clusters when the merge/sort package is run. This feature effectively bunches all transactions with identical patient IDs into adjacent records, thus making posting and statement generation easy.

Figure 7.7 outlines the transaction program. As before, each entry is stored in a random file with an index subfile. The index may be sorted with merge/sort and then used to access the transactions in order, producing the file shown in Fig. 7.9.

The transaction header record is updated so that subsequent transactions may be added to the end of the file. Dr. Goode's staff is to enter transactions any time they want without restarting or searching for the end of the files.

In Fig. 7.8, the transaction program is developed in greater detail. In step 3.3, for example, the system asks if the transaction is a payment or charge. In case it is a payment, the sign of the amount entered is set to minus so that the payment amount is deducted from the balance.

A sample run of the transaction system is shown in Fig. 7.9. The patient ID is needed as a key to each record. The record number is shown as a check, and the audit trail date is printed along with the transaction description. The charge or payment is also displayed for checking purposes.

1. PROGRAM: Build a Transaction File Along With Its Index Subfile

2. DATA:

I = patient ID number, initially input
A$ = audit trail date of transaction, initially input
C$ = statement comment for billing explanation, initially input
B = amount charged or paid, initially input
P1 = check sum of balances, initially input
P2 = check sum of transactions, initially input
S1 = beginning record number of transaction file, initially input
T1 = total number of master file records, initially input
S = sign of amount: (-1) if payment, $(+1)$ if charge

3. STEPS:

3.1. Open #1 as "TRANS"
      #2 as "ITRANS"
3.2. Read TRANSACTION header record
3.3. Input "Is this a payment?"
      If "yes" then set $S = (-1)$
      If "not yes" then set $S = (+1)$
3.4. Input I
      If I=0 then stop (step 3.12)
      Otherwise continue
3.5. Input A$, C$, B
3.6. Let $B = S \cdot B$; calculate P2 check sum
3.7. Write #1, I, A$, C$, B as record S1
3.8. Write #2, I, S1
3.9. Increment S1
3.10. Print listing: I, A$, C$, B, S1
3.11. Goto step 3.3
3.12. Update transaction header: S1, P2, P1, T1
3.13. Close Files

Fig. 7.8 BLUE$_1$ for the transaction file input

The probes shown in the last line of Fig. 7.10 give the next record number (9), the total dollar value of the transactions (645), and the total dollar value of the master file at this time (70). The number of master file records is also kept (5).

The BASIC program of Fig. 7.10 is straightforward for the most part. Lines 150 to 165 are tricky, and we should study them with extra effort. The RESTORE #1 command positions the record pointer to record number zero. In line 150, this allows update of the transaction header record. In line 160, however, the RESTORE #1 is used to prevent an End-Of-File marker from being written when the END #1 command is executed. Since this peculiarity may not exist in some personal computers, be sure to watch for this in line 160.

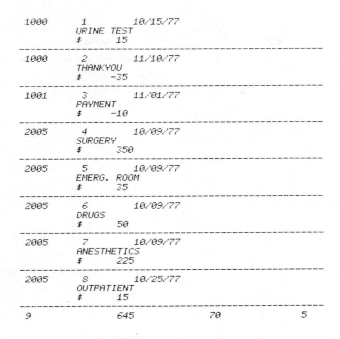

```
1000        1         10/15/77
          URINE TEST
          $      15
---------------------------------------------------------
1000        2         11/10/77
          THANKYOU
          $     -35
---------------------------------------------------------
1001        3         11/01/77
          PAYMENT
          $     -10
---------------------------------------------------------
2005        4         10/09/77
          SURGERY
          $     350
---------------------------------------------------------
2005        5         10/09/77
          EMERG. ROOM
          $      35
---------------------------------------------------------
2005        6         10/09/77
          DRUGS
          $    50
---------------------------------------------------------
2005        7         10/09/77
          ANESTHETICS
          $     225
---------------------------------------------------------
2005        8         10/25/77
          OUTPATIENT
          $      15
---------------------------------------------------------
  9                  645              70              5
```

Fig. 7.9 Sample run output from transaction program

Statement Generation

The posting and statement generation routine must accomplish the following:

1. Merge transactions with master records
2. Compute balances
3. Print a statement for each active account
4. Update the master records
5. Reset the transaction header

These steps are accomplished in the $BLUE_0$ specification of Fig. 7.11 and the detailed specification plan of Fig. 7.12.

Briefly, the blueprints illustrate the treacherous merge process that we studied in Chap. 4. The transaction file is read and the master file is searched until a match in patient ID occurs. The search relies upon a *sequential scan* of the *ordered* file. If the transaction record is out of order or simply does not match the master file, it is written into an error file called "ERROR."

```
  5 LET D=4
 10 REM  ******************************************************************
 11 REM              A/R TRANSACTION BUILD PROGRAM
 12 REM                    COPYRIGHT 1977
 13 REM  ******************************************************************
 20 DIM A$[8], C$[16], Y$[1]
 29 REM  ----------------------------------------------------------------
 30 OPEN#1, "TRANS"
 31 OPEN#2, "ITRANS"
 34 REM  ----------------------------------------------------------------
 35 RESTORE#1
 36 INPUT#1, S1, P2, P1, T1
 38 REM  ----------------------------------------------------------------
 40 PRINT "IS THIS A PAYMENT(P), OR A CHARGE(C) ?"; INPUT Y$
 45 IF Y$="P" THEN 55
 50 IF Y$="C" THEN 60
 52 GOTO 40
 55 LET S=(-1); GOTO 70
 60 LET S=(1)
 69 REM  ----------------------------------------------------------------
 70 PRINT "PATIENT ID                :"; INPUT I
 71 IF I=0 THEN 150
 72 PRINT "DATE OF TRANSACT. MM/DD/YY: "; INPUT A$
 73 PRINT "COMMENT (MAXIMUM OF 16 )  :"; INPUT C$
 74 PRINT "AMOUNT                   $"; INPUT B
 79 REM  ----------------------------------------------------------------
 81 LET B=S*B; LET P2=P2+B
 85 REM  ----------------------------------------------------------------
 87 RESTORE#1, S1
 90 PRINT#1, I, "I", A$, C$, B
 95 RESTORE#2, S1-1
100 PRINT#2, I, S1
105 REM  ----------------------------------------------------------------
110 LET S1=S1+1
115 REM  ----------------------------------------------------------------
120 PRINT#D, I, TAB(10), S1-1, TAB(20), A$
125 PRINT#D, TAB(10), C$
130 PRINT#D, TAB(10), "$", B
135 PRINT#D, "-------------------------------------------------------------"
139 REM  ----------------------------------------------------------------
140 GOTO 40
150 RESTORE#1
155 PRINT#1, S1, P2, P1, T1
157 PRINT#D, S1, P2, P1, T1
159 REM  ----------------------------------------------------------------
160 RESTORE#1
161 END#1
165 END#2
169 REM  ----------------------------------------------------------------
170 RETURN
```

Fig. 7.10 BLUE$_2$ for transaction file input program

When all corresponding transactions have been read for a given master record, the master record is updated and signed with the new date. Displaying the master file would reveal the date of the last posting.

Finally, the transaction file is copied into the error file in the event that the number of transactions exceed the number of active accounts in the master file.

Figure 7.13 is the BASIC refinement for the A/R posting subprogram. It is easily understood after reading the blueprints in Figs. 7.11

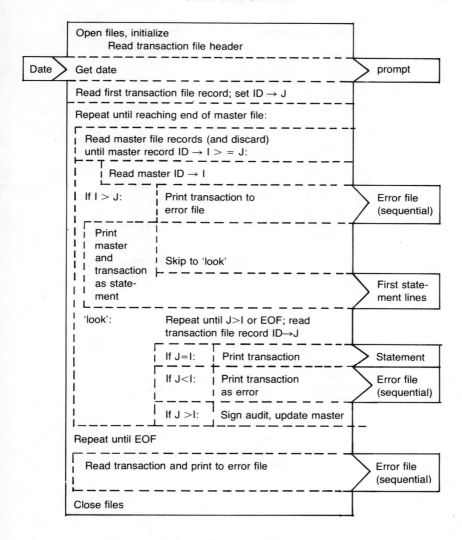

Fig. 7.11 BLUE$_0$ for statement generation and posting routine

and 7.12. Again, pay particular attention to the file commands and how separators are used to separate character strings with digits from numbers with digits.

Licking the Envelopes

Once the posting program is run, the statements have been produced and we only need to lick the envelopes and mail them. We can even avoid a sticky tongue if a sealed mailer is used.

1. PROGRAM:　Statements and Posting of Master/Transaction Files

2. DATE:
   I　 = master file ID, initially input
   J　 = transaction file ID, initially input
   N$ = master file name, initially input
   S$ = master file street, initially input
   C$ = master file city, initially input
   Z　 = Zip code, initially input
   D$ = statement transaction comment, initially input
   B1 = master file balance, initially input
   B2 = transaction file amount, initially input
   A$ = transaction file audit trail date, initially input
   U$ = master file audit trail date, initially input
   P$ = phone number, initially input
   P1 = check sum of master file balances, initially input
   P2 = check sum of transaction amounts, initially input
   S1 = total number of transaction records, initially input
   T1 = total number of master records, initially input
   K　 = record number of transaction file, initially one

3. STEPS:
   3.1. Open #1 as "MASTER"
   　　　　　#2 as "TRANS"
   　　　　　#3 as "ERROR"
   3.2. Read transaction header: S1, P2, P1, T1
   　　　If S1<=1 then stop (3.8)
   　　　Read transaction record: J, A$, D$, B2
   3.3. Input signature date for Master audit trail, U$
   3.4. Repeat T1 times
   　　　　　3.4.1. Read master file, ID→I
   　　　　　　　　　　　If I<J then goto end of loop (3.4.4)
   　　　　　3.4.2. If I>J then Print #3, J, A$, D$, B2
   　　　　　　　　　　Goto 'look' (3.4.3)
   　　　　　　　　　　Print statement header information
   　　　　　　　　　　Print I, N$, S$, C$, Z, P$, B1
   　　　　　　　　　　Compute probes: P1 = P1−B2
   　　　　　　　　　　　　　　　　　　　　P2 = P2−B2
   　　　　　3.4.3. 'look': If S1 = 0 then 'break out of look'
   　　　　　　　　　　Read transaction: J, A$, D$, B2
   　　　　　　　　　　Decrement count S1-(S1-1)
   　　　　　　　　　　If J=I print: J, A$, D$, B2
   　　　　　　　　　　Adjust probes: P2 = P2−B2
   　　　　　　　　　　　　　　　　　　　P1 = P1−B2
   　　　　　　　　　　Goto 'look'
   　　　　　　　　　　If J<1 print #3, J, A$, D$, B2
   　　　　　　　　　　Adjust probes: P2 = P2−B2
   　　　　　　　　　　　　　　　　　　　P1 = P1−B2
   　　　　　　　　　　Goto 'look'
   　　　　　3.4.4. If J>1 update master file balance

Fig. 7.12　BLUE₁ for statement generation and posting

    3.5. Repeat until end of transaction file
          Read #2, J, A$, D$, B2
          Print #3, J, A$, D$, B2
          Adjust probes: P2 = P2−B2
    3.6. Update transaction header: S1, P2, P1, T1
    3.7. Print probes
    3.8. Close #1, #2, #3

Fig. 7.12 Continued

```
5 LET D=4
10 REM ******************************************************************
11 REM                      A/R POSTING PROGRAM
12 REM                       COPYRIGHT 1977
13 REM ******************************************************************
20 DIM N$[16], S$[16], C$[16], P$[12], A$[8], D$[16], U$[8], X$[1]
22 REM ---------------------------------------------------------------
30 OPEN#1, "MASTER"
31 OPEN#2, "TRANS"
32 OPEN#3, "ERROR"
35 REM ---------------------------------------------------------------
40 RESTORE#2
42 INPUT#2, S1; P2; P1; T1
44 IF S1<=1 THEN 210
46 RESTORE#2, 1
47 INPUT#2, J; X$; A$; D$; B2
48 LET K=2; LET S1=S1-1
49 REM ---------------------------------------------------------------
50 PRINT "ENTER DATE MM/DD/YY        : "; INPUT U$
55 REM ---------------------------------------------------------------
60 FOR K1=0 TO T1-1
65 RESTORE#1, K1
70 INPUT#1, I; N$; S$; C$; Z; X$; P$; B1
75 IF I<J THEN 160
79 REM ---------------------------------------------------------------
80 IF I=J THEN 90
83 PRINT#3, J; "J"; A$; D$; B2
84 LET P2=P2-B2
85 GOTO 110
86 REM ---------------------------------------------------------------
90 PRINT#D
91 PRINT#D, TAB(10), I
92 PRINT#D, TAB(10), N$, TAB(28), " FAMILY", TAB(40), P$
93 PRINT#D, TAB(10), S$
94 PRINT#D, TAB(10), C$, TAB(30), Z
95 PRINT#D, TAB(50), "$", B1
96 PRINT#D, TAB(10), A$, TAB(25), D$, TAB(50), "$", B2
99 REM ---------------------------------------------------------------
100 LET P1=P1+B2; LET B1=B1+B2; LET P2=P2-B2
102 REM ---------------------------------------------------------------
110 REM       LOOK
111 IF S1=1 THEN 150
112 RESTORE#2, K
114 INPUT#2, J; X$; A$; D$; B2
116 LET K=K+1; LET S1=S1-1
118 REM ---------------------------------------------------------------
120 IF J#I THEN 140
124 LET P1=P1+B2; LET B1=B1+B2; LET P2=P2-B2
125 IF J#I THEN 140
```

Fig. 7.13 BLUE$_2$ specification for posting program

```
130 PRINT#D, TAB(10), A$, TAB(25), D$, TAB(50), "$", B2
138 GOTO 110
139 REM ------------------------------------------------------------
140 IF J>I THEN 150
145 PRINT#3, J, "J"; A$; D$; B2
148 GOTO 110
149 REM ------------------------------------------------------------
150 RESTORE#1, K1
151 PRINT#1, I; N$; S$; C$; Z; "Z"; P$; B1; "B"; U$
153 PRINT#D, TAB(42), "BALANCE $", B1
158 REM ------------------------------------------------------------
160 NEXT K1
169 REM ------------------------------------------------------------
170 IF S1=1 THEN 200
175 RESTORE#2, K
180 INPUT#2, J; X$; A$; D$; B2
185 LET K=K+1; LET S1=S1-1
190 PRINT#3, J, "J"; A$; D$; B2
192 LET P2=P2-B2
195 GOTO 170
199 REM ------------------------------------------------------------
200 RESTORE#2
202 REM PRINT#2, S1; P1; P2; T1
203 REM ------------------------------------------------------------
205 PRINT#D, "PROBE, MASTER CHECKSUM=", P1
206 PRINT#D, "PROBE, TRANSACTION CHECKSUM=", P2
209 REM ------------------------------------------------------------
210 END#1
211 RESTORE#2
212 END#2
213 END#3
220 RETURN
```

Fig. 7.13   Continued

In any case, the output from the BASIC posting and statement generation program is shown in Fig. 7.14.

Each statement contains an address and pertinent information about the patient. The starting balance is printed followed by a listing of the transactions. The final balance is printed, and this is the amount owed the clinic.

The check sum probes give the total amount remaining "on the books" at this time. Thus, Dr. Goode's clinic is floating $715 in receivables, according to Fig. 7.14. The transaction probe should be zero, indicating that all transactions were either processed or written to the error file.

This system does not include aged accounting. If it did, then the transactions would be aged over 60, 90, or 120 plus days. The aged accounts could then be flagged for collection duty. This feature is very important to an A/R system. Its implementation is left as an exercise.

The A/R system is implemented in separate modules. Actually, it may be necessary to break a large system into smaller parts because of main memory limitations. We could have *overlayed* main memory by appending the appropriate program to a monitor program, as shown in Fig. 7.15.

```
     1000
  G. K. BARNES        FAMILY       503-928-4086
  4895 MEEKER
  ALBANY, OR.            97321
                                          $             35
  10/15/77          URINE TEST          $             15
  11/10/77          THANKYOU            $            -35
                                  BALANCE $            15

     1001
  T. G. LEWIS         FAMILY       503-258-4195
  57 E. ISABELLA
  LEBANON, OR.          97355
                                          $             10
  11/01/77          PAYMENT             $            -10
                                  BALANCE $             0

     2005
  CATFISH DAVE        FAMILY       503-555-1212
  451 SW. OAK
  SWEETWATER, OR.       97400
                                          $             25
  10/09/77          SURGERY             $            350
  10/09/77          EMERG. ROOM         $             35
  10/09/77          DRUGS               $             50
  10/09/77          ANESTHETICS         $            225
  10/25/77          OUTPATIENT          $             15
                                  BALANCE $            700
PROBE, MASTER CHECKSUM=            715
PROBE, TRANSACTION CHECKSUM=         0
```

Fig. 7.14 Output from posting program: statements

The APP command is useful for overlaying one program onto another. The temporary overlay provides a way to share memory and run large programs piece-by-piece. The files in Fig. 7.15 are BASic files on DRive #1.

A final comment: The system described here could have been implemented in a variety of ways. The hashing function technique could have been used throughout, for example. Also, the posting routine could have been written for sequential files rather than random files. We turn now to only one possible alternative solution.

```
1 PRINT "SELECT (1, 2, OR 3) FROM MENU :"
2 PRINT "1. CREATE MASTER ACCOUNT FILE."
3 PRINT "2. CREATE/ADD TO TRANSACTIONS."
4 PRINT "3. POST AND BILLING RUN."
5 PRINT "ENTER ?", INPUT N9
6 IF N9=1 THEN 10
7 IF N9=2 THEN 20
8 IF N9=3 THEN 30
9 GOTO 1
10 APP "ARMASTER/BAS.DR1"
20 APP "ARTRANS/BAS.DR1"
30 APP "ARPOST/BAS.DR1"
```

Fig. 7.15 Overlay monitor program

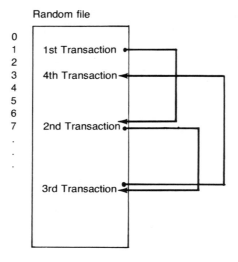

Fig. 7.16 A linked list transaction file

The Second Solution: Linked Lists

A modification to the transaction file is possible where sorting may be avoided. This method uses a linked list structure illustrated in Fig. 7.16. The advantage of this approach is that no time is lost due to sorting, and more importantly, no additional space is needed for the sort files.

The Transaction File

The transaction file is a collection of records, as shown in Fig. 7.16. Each record contains the information included before, plus a field called the *link*. A link is a number that gives the random access position of a subsequent transaction record with the same patient ID key.

The file is constructed using a hashing function to locate the first transaction. Once the first transaction is found, the link field gives the location of the second transaction, and so forth. Finally, the last transaction is found, the statement is generated.

Each statement is produced from one master file record and a linked list of transactions. Therefore, it is not necessary to sort the transaction file in order to cluster transactions with matching patient ID.

What, No Sort/Merge?

Nope!

Linked list techniques are most useful for on-line, interactive systems. We could have designed the A/R system with on-line capability. This would have required the updating of each master record immediately after each transaction was entered. The balance in the master record would be up-to-date, but the amount of processing would also be greater. These systems require greater diskette speed, which is accomplished with high-speed cartridge disks.

Chapter Eight

AMBITIOUS ARNOLD'S ACCOUNTING AGENCY

A FABLE: Once upon a time, a young man went for a walk in the dark woods. He became lost, and when nightfall arrived, he built a shelter, lit a fire, and searched for food. Days passed into years, and his shelter became a comfortable place to live. Finally, after five years, he was found by a party of fur trappers. He excitedly returned to civilization in anticipation of hot baths, buildings, and the friends he had left behind. But he did not live happily ever after, and as he grew older, he realized his place was back in the woods. Returning, he again began to build a wilderness life.

ANOTHER FABLE: Once upon a time there was a young electronics engineer. He purchased a Citizens Band radio kit and began putting the pieces together. As the years passed, he built twenty electronics kits in his spare time. In fact, he also made many improvements in the systems he constructed, and, to his surprise, others became interested in his techniques. Finally, after five years, he became a successful mail order supplier of electronic kits. His family moved into a big house on a hill, and he became so busy with business that he never got the chance to work on his own kits. As he grew older, he realized his place was back in the garage next to his tools. Selling his successful mail order house, he returned to the simple life of a hobby kit builder.

MORAL: It's the going, not the getting there, that's good.

Arnold Heroda was born and raised near the lava flows of Hilo, Hawaii. He spent days of his life playing in the volcanic ash with his Japanese cousins. Those were the good old days.

As Arnold grew up, he learned the value of discipline and earnest effort. His grandmother would tell him stories about the ancient Japanese warriors and their pride. She also reminded him of the days during World War II when his mother, father, and all their Japanese friends were moved to concentration camps because of fear. Arnold learned that nothing in this world could be guaranteed.

130

Arnold was ambitious. He was easy-going and happy most of the time, but he was above all else ambitious. By the time he went to high school, Arnold had managed to save enough money for a car. He had also earned two speeding tickets before he was old enough to drive.

In high school, Arnold sold and rented surf boards to the tourists on Waikiki. His parents moved to Honolulu just to be with Arnold.

His first venture into the real world came two days after graduating from school. Arnold opened a sidewalk stand in the middle of Ala Moana Shopping Center to sell frozen yogurt. This enterprise earned Arnold enough money to get started in another high-profit venture near the beach. Arnold opened one of the first adult book shops in the islands.

Soon Arnold owned a small chain of adult book shops specializing in local folk lore and special sand-based perfumes. His adult book shops were doing very well indeed when Arnold decided to go into business with two brothers who were friends of his, Sugar Cane and Willing N. Able.

The partners opened an accounting agency that worked with businesses in Honolulu. They provided general ledger, payroll, taxes, and consulting services for the restaurants, hotels, and tourist shops around Waikiki. The agency was, like all other ventures attempted by Arnold, extremely successful.

Arnold promised himself a wife and devised a plan and schedule to work toward that goal. On July 15th, he would make it a point to meet at least three young ladies. By August 15th, he intended to narrow the selection to one lucky wahine. His schedule called for a Christmas wedding and a family of average size by the end of the first four years of marriage. Arnold, needless to say, was very methodical.

The marriage plan was carried out with great precision and success. Arnold completed the courtship, marriage, and ended up with a slightly larger family than the national average of 1.8 offspring. Arnold's two sons were named Adolph and Albert.

Everything went fine for a while. Unfortunately, Arnold realized too late that his bride was fond of running things. To be frank, Arnold was henpecked. Furthermore, Adolph and Albert were spoiled and undisciplined. Arnold was losing ground rapidly.

After work, Arnold would retire in front of the TV to watch "Five-O" or the news. This was a time when he could relax and enjoy some peace and quiet. Recently, however, he had become annoyed by interruptions from Adolph, Albert, and his wife. They either wanted to watch a different channel, or they wanted him to fix the plumbing. Arnold was being deprived of his last form of enjoyment. It was time for him to strike back.

To ward off his wife and two sons, Arnold devised an elaborate plan called "Peace Plan I." The strategy employed against his wife was a secret (hence it cannot be told), but it worked. To ward off his two unruly sons, Arnold invested in an electronic game. He purchased a personal computer fully equipped with a games tape.

Adolph and Albert spent hours playing Star Trek on their new toy. Their mother began sewing and preparing for their new baby, and Arnold relaxed in front of the family TV with a can of beer. At long last peace, or was it?

Arnold was about to drop off to sleep when he lunged forward in his easy chair. He was struck with an idea as devastating to Peace Plan I as a bolt of lightning. Why not do his own household accounting on the kids' new toy? In fact, couldn't Arnold accomplish even greater peace of mind by computerizing his budget? Furthermore, Adolph and Albert could do the programming and save Arnold a lot of work.

Arnold's Household Budget

Designing the Chart-of-Accounts

Arnold plunged into the design of his household budget system like a busman on holiday. His first step was to design a chart-of-accounts showing each category of income and expense. The next steps included designing the input formats to his sons' personal computer and deciding how to accrue the income and expense items. Arnold rolled up his sleeves and jotted down the things he needed to do.

1. Design a chart-of-accounts for a household budget.
2. Design and implement a program to input the chart-of-accounts file along with year-to-date totals and monthly budget amounts.
3. Run the chart program and input the chart-of-accounts data.
4. Design a transaction file (input) to take check stub information and input it into the computer. The computer will then print an income statement and net gain or loss for each month.
5. Design and implement the processing program needed in step 4.

Arnold designed the chart-of-accounts for a typical household. He tried it for his own household and then he used it to budget the author's household, as shown in Fig. 8.1.

The chart of Fig. 8.1 shows several techniques invented by Arnold to make his system flexible. First, the accounts are numbered for reference later by the processing program. Item 100 is a heading for the INCOME accounts. The code "T" is used to mean title.

```
CHART-OF-ACCOUNTS FILE    :        LEWIS

ACCT: CODE:       TITLE          BUDGET      YEAR-TO-DATE      CURRENT MO.

  100   T        INCOME
  101   + NET PAYCHECK          $   600    $        0$              0
  102   + PUBLISHERS ROYALTIES  $   250    $        0$              0
  199   S TOTAL INCOME          $   850    $        0$              0


  200   T        EXPENSES
  201   + FOOD                  $   200    $        0$              0
  202   + HOUSING               $   275    $        0$              0
  300   + CLOTHING              $    85    $        0$              0
  400   + TRANSPORTATION        $    75    $        0$              0
  500   + PERSONAL              $    55    $        0$              0
  600   + EDUCATION             $    25    $        0$              0
  601   + RECREATION            $    60    $        0$              0
  701   + MEDICAL               $    20    $        0$              0
  801   + SAVINGS               $    25    $        0$              0
  900   + MISCELLANEOUS         $    30    $        0$              0
  999   S TOTAL EXPENSES        $   850    $        0$              0
```

Fig. 8.1 Chart-of-accounts file for Lewis

Second, every account has an action code of either T (title), + (add to total), or S (sum the items from a previous T). Thus, the two income accounts of Fig. 8.1 are totaled by account item 199.

The chart also contains an amount budgeted by the user. In the beginning, the year-to-date amount is zero, but as the months pass by, and additional transactions are added to last (previous) month's balance, the year-to-date total increases.

The final item stored in the chart-of-accounts file is the current month's total for each item.

The Chart Program Blueprints

Figure 8.2 illustrates the blueprints for Arnold's household budget system of accounts. The user inputs a name used to open a file. This file will contain the chart-of-accounts for the life of the system. This system is used to produce the output of Fig. 8.1.

The blueprints of Fig. 8.2 show that a simple sequential file is needed to store the chart information. Since all processing will be by serial access to the chart-of-accounts, a sequential file is sufficient. Arnold was able to use the tape drive subsystem that Adolph and Albert used for their games.

The second level blueprint of Fig. 8.2(B) shows how Arnold incorporated check sum probes (T1, T2, T3) for error control and also used them to print out subtotals. Thus the chart-of-accounts subsystem is self-checking. Other techniques are often used by accountants such as audit trail signatures (see Chap. 5), but Arnold didn't feel that they were needed.

(A) BLUE₀

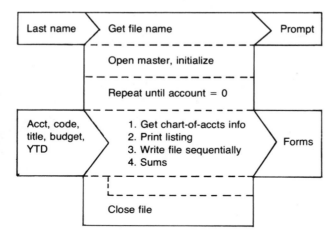

(B) BLUE₁

1. PROGRAM:　Chart-of-Accounts Master File

2. DATA:

　　　　　F$ = family name used for master file name, input
　　　　　A = account number, input
　　　　　C$ = action code, input
　　　　　T$ = title or description, input
　　　　　B = monthly budget, input
　　　　　Y = year-to-date total, input
　T1, T2, T3) = running totals for budget, year-to-date, and current month, initially zero
E1, E2, E3)
　　　　　M = current month amount, always zero

3. STEPS:

　　　3.1.　Get F$
　　　3.2.　Open #1, F$; set T1=T2=T3=M=0
　　　3.3 　Repeat
　　　　　　Input A
　　　　　　If A=0 stop
　　　　　　Input C$, T$, B, Y
　　　　　　Write #1, A, C$, T$, "$", B, "$", Y, "$", M
　　　　　　If C$ = "T" then skip to print
　　　　　　If C$ = "S" then skip to total
　　　　　　Sums: T1=T1 + B; T2=T2 + Y; T3=T3 + M
　　　　　　Print A, C$, T$, B, Y, M
　　　　　　GOTO 3.3
　　print:　Print A, C$, T$
　　　　　　GOTO 3.3

Fig. 8.2　BLUE specifications for chart-of-accounts programs

```
total:  Print A, C$, T$, T1, T2, T3
        Let E1=T1; E2=T2, E3=T3
        Set T1=T2=T3=0
        Go to 3.3
3.4.    Close #1
```

Fig. 8.2 Continued

```
10 LET D=4
100 REM  ************************************************************
101 REM                    CHART OF ACCOUNTS PROGRAM
102 REM                        COPYRIGHT 1977
103 REM  ************************************************************
110 DIM F$[8], C$[1], T$[20], K$[3]
112 REM -----------------------------------------------------------
120 PRINT "ENTER THE INPUT FILE NAME (8) : "; INPUT F$
121 PRINT#D, "CHART-OF-ACCOUNTS FILE    : ", F$
122 PRINT#D
124 REM -----------------------------------------------------------
130 OPEN#1, F$
135 LET T1=0; T2=0; T3=0; M=0
136 PRINT#D, "ACCT: CODE:      TITLE", TAB(30), "BUDGET", TAB(40), "YEAR-TO-DATE";
137 PRINT#D, TAB(55), "CURRENT MO. "
139 REM -----------------------------------------------------------
140 PRINT "ACCOUNT (3 DIGITS)        : "; INPUT A
150 IF A=0 THEN 230
160 PRINT "ACTION CODE (T, S, OR +)  : "; INPUT C$
162 PRINT "TITLE (20 CHAR. MAX)      : "; INPUT T$
164 PRINT "BUDGET AMOUNT            $"; INPUT B
166 PRINT "YEAR-TO-DATE AMOUNT      $"; INPUT Y
168 PRINT
170 PRINT "ENTRIES, OK               ?"; INPUT K$
172 IF K$="NO" THEN 140
175 REM -----------------------------------------------------------
180 PRINT#1, A; C$; T$; "$"; B; "$"; Y; "M"
185 IF C$="T" THEN 210
190 IF C$="S" THEN 220
200 REM ------------------SUMS------------------------------------
202 LET T1=T1+B; T2=T2+Y; T3=T3+M
205 PRINT#D, A, TAB(6), C$, TAB(8), T$, TAB(30), "$", B, TAB(40), "$", Y, TAB(50), "$", M
207 GOTO 140
209 REM-----------------PRINT----------------------------------
210 PRINT#D
212 PRINT#D, A, TAB(6), C$, TAB(8), T$
215 GOTO 140
219 REM -----------------TOTAL----------------------------------
220 PRINT#D, A, TAB(6), C$, TAB(8), T$, TAB(30), "$", T1, TAB(40), "$", T2, TAB(50), "$", T3
221 PRINT#D
222 LET E1=T1; E2=T2; E3=T3
224 LET T1=0; T2=0; T3=0
226 GOTO 140
229 REM -----------------WHOA----------------------------------
230 END#1
250 END
```

Fig. 8.3 BASIC program for chart-of-accounts

The BASIC program of Fig. 8.3 is a straightforward application of the blueprints. Lines 136, 137 and lines 220, 221 are actually a single PRINT #D statement, but they have been split into two because of their length.

Lines 140 to 170 serve as prompting for operator lead through. In line 150, the user is given the option of continuing or stopping. In line 172, the operator is given a choice of continuing or correcting an input error.

The Transaction Process

Arnold's Check Stubs

Arnold's accounting subsystem is designed to work together with the family check book. At the end of each month, Adolph enters the date, check number, purpose of check, and amount of check into the computer along with the account number. This transaction is added to the appropriate account number contained in the chart-of-accounts file. Thus, each transaction is placed in the correct category and summed to obtain a subtotal.

Figure 8.4 illustrates the use of the transaction processor devised by Arnold and used to process the author's July budget. This first run is called the income statement and shows each check written along with the date and amount.

In Fig. 8.4, the title (item 100) is used to help read the statement. Item 101 has a beginning balance shown by the first NET PAYCHECK title. The last NET PAYCHECK title follows the vertical dotted line and contains the year-to-date total and current month total.

The account transactions for account number 101 show how little teaching pays even though payday is twice per month. The university issues a check numbered 96 on the first and fifteenth of each month.

Item 102 is shown as income on the 25th from Hayden Books. The royalty of $230 was $20 under the budgeted amount of $250.

The sum of items in line 201 shows that in July the family spent $172.54 on food, even though the budget allowed a $200 investment. This total was obtained from three checks, one written to Safeway, one to the A&P, and one written to the Minimart for a keg of beer.

The totals printed at the bottom of the income statement of Fig. 8.4 show a surplus balance of $53.61 for the month. This fortunate circumstance occurred because the family stayed home all month and spent very little on health, education, or welfare.

```
CHART OF ACCOUNTS FOR FILE :     LEWIS
OUTPUT CHART OF ACCOUNTS FILE :  JULY
ACCT:CODE:     TITLE              BUDGET     YEAR-TO-DATE     CURRENT MO.

100   T          INCOME
101   + NET PAYCHECK            $  600     $        0$              0
101     07/01  96      TEACHING                     $            300
```

Fig. 8.4   First run of transaction processing for Lewis

```
101     07/15  96    TEACHING                              $              300
-----------------------------------------------------------------------------
101   + NET PAYCHECK             $   600   $      600$     600

102   + PUBLISHERS ROYALTIES  $   250   $        0$     0
102     07/25  32    HAYDEN BOOKS                          $              230
-----------------------------------------------------------------------------
102   + PUBLISHERS ROYALTIES  $   250   $      230$     230

199   S TOTAL INCOME             $   850   $      830$     830

200   T       EXPENSES
201   + FOOD                     $   200   $        0$     0
201     07/11  172   SAFEWAYS                              $              52.11
201     07/24  191   A&P                                   $              98.35
201     07/16  168   MINIMART                              $              22.08
-----------------------------------------------------------------------------
201   + FOOD                     $   200   $    172.54$    172.54

202   + HOUSING                  $   275   $        0$     0
202     07/10  149   RENT                                  $              275
202     07/18  205   UTILITIES                             $              75.3
202     07/25  210   TELEPHONE                             $              30.55
-----------------------------------------------------------------------------
202   + HOUSING                  $   275   $    380.85$    380.85

300   + CLOTHING                 $    85   $        0$     0
300     07/08  130   MADELINE CLOTHES                      $              48
-----------------------------------------------------------------------------
300   + CLOTHING                 $    85   $       48$     48

400   + TRANSPORTATION           $    75   $        0$     0
400     07/12  170   CAR PAYMT                             $              125
-----------------------------------------------------------------------------
400   + TRANSPORTATION           $    75   $      125$     125

500   + PERSONAL                 $    55   $        0$     0
-----------------------------------------------------------------------------
500   + PERSONAL                 $    55   $        0$     0

600   + EDUCATION                $    25   $        0$     0
-----------------------------------------------------------------------------
600   + EDUCATION                $    25   $        0$     0

601   + RECREATION               $    60   $        0$     0
-----------------------------------------------------------------------------
601   + RECREATION               $    60   $        0$     0

701   + MEDICAL                  $    20   $        0$     0
-----------------------------------------------------------------------------
701   + MEDICAL                  $    20   $        0$     0

801   + SAVINGS                  $    25   $        0$     0
801     07/30  200   CREDIT UNION                          $              35
-----------------------------------------------------------------------------
801   + SAVINGS                  $    25   $       35$     35

900   + MISCELLANEOUS            $    30   $        0$     0


900     07/21  160   BABYSITTER                            $              15
-----------------------------------------------------------------------------
900   + MISCELLANEOUS            $    30   $       15$     15

999   S TOTAL  EXPENSES          $   850   $    776.39$    776.39
          INCOME - EXPENSES :  $     0   $     53.61$    53.61
```

Fig. 8.4 Continued

The Transaction Process Blueprints

Arnold's household budget system works on the basis of check stubs collected during the month. When Arnold wants to enter the amounts from his check book, he must execute the program blueprinted in Fig. 8.5.

This system reads each account from the chart-of-accounts file and asks the user if there are any transactions with account number A to be entered. If the answer is "yes," then the date, check number, description, and amount are entered.

The old chart-of-accounts file is ignored after the transactions are processed. The output is to a new file containing updated informa-

(A) BLUE₀

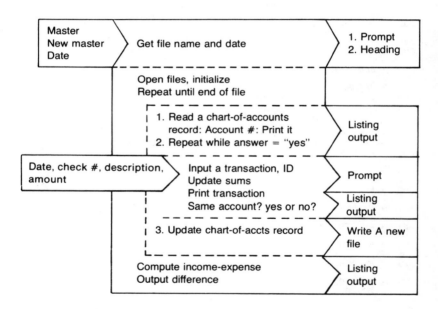

(B) BLUE₁

1. PROGRAM: Process the Budget Entries

2. DATA:

        F$ = input master, file name, input
        E$ = output master, file name, input
        A   = account number, input
        C$ = action code, input
        T$ = title, input

Fig. 8.5 BLUE specification for budget program

B = monthly budget, input
Y = year-to-date total
T1, T2, T3 = budget, year-to-date, and current month totals, input
E1, E2, E3 = totals for income, initially unknown
S2, S3 = year-to-date and current transaction totals, computed
A1 = transaction account number, input
D$ = date of transaction, input
K$ = check number of transaction, input
U$ = description of transaction, input
M = current month amount, input
X$ = a one character spacer between fields in the master file, initially unknown
Y$ = "yes" or "no" answer, input

3. STEPS:
   3.1. Get F$, E$
   3.2. Open #1, F$, open #2, E$
      Initialize T1=T2=T3=0, set stop flag W=0
   3.3. Read #1, A, C$, T$, X$, B, X$, Y, X$, M
      3.3.1. If EOF #1 then skip to 3.4
           Set S2=Y, S3=0 transaction sums
           If C$="T" then skip to print 3.3.3
           If C$="s" then skip to total 3.3.4
           Print #D, A, C$, T$, B, Y, M
      3.3.2. Print "Do you have more account,"
           A, "S to enter?", Y$
           If Y$ = "No" then goto 3.3.6
           If Y$ = "Yes" then goto 3.3.5
           Goto 3.3.2
      3.3.3. Print: print A, C$, T$, then go to 3.3.6
      3.3.4. Total: print A, C$, T$, T1, T2, T3
           If W=1 then skip to 3.4
           Set W=1
           Write next month's chart of accounts file to device #2
           Let E1=T1, E2=T2, E3=T3
           Let T1=T2=T3=0
           Goto 3.3
      3.3.5. Get a transaction, input A1, D$, K$, U$, M
           Let S2=S2+M; S3-S3+M
           Print #D, A1, D$, K$, U$, TAB, S2, S3
           Goto 3.3.2
      3.3.6. Update chart:
           Write #2, A, C$, T$, "$", B, "$", S2, "$", 0.00
           If C$="+" then goto 3.3
           Otherwise print transaction sums: A, C$, T$, B, S2, S3
           Set T1=T1+B, T2=T2+S2, T3=T3+S3
           Goto 3.3
   3.4. Compute income −expenses
      Since W=1 we are done
      T1=E1−T1; T2=E2−T2; T3=E3−T3
      Print #D; "Income −Expenses:"; T1, T2, T3
   3.5. Close #1, #2

Fig. 8.5 Continued

```
900 LET D=4
1000 REM ******************************************************************
1001 REM                      PROCESS TRANSACTIONS
1002 REM                        COPYRIGHT 1977
1003 REM ******************************************************************
1010 DIM F$[8], E$[8], C$[1], T$[20], D$[5], K$[3], U$[20], Y$[3], X$[1]
1012 REM -----------------------------------------------------------------
1020 PRINT "ENTER CHART OF ACCOUNTS FILE NAME  : "; INPUT F$
1022 PRINT#D, "CHART OF ACCOUNTS FOR FILE  : ", F$
1025 PRINT "ENTER OUTPUT CHART OF ACCOUNTS FILE NAME  : "; INPUT E$
1026 PRINT#D, "OUTPUT CHART OF ACCOUNTS FILE  : ", E$
1027 PRINT#D, "ACCT CODE:       TITLE", TAB(30), "BUDGET", TAB(40), "YEAR-TO-DATE";
1028 PRINT#D, TAB(55), "CURRENT MO. "
1029 REM -----------------------------------------------------------------
1030 OPEN#1, F$
1032 OPEN#2, E$
1034 LET T1=0; T2=0; T3=0; W=0
1035 REM -----------------------LOOP-------------------------------------
1040 INPUT#1, A; C$; T$; X$; B; X$; Y; X$; M
1041 IF EOF#1 THEN 1160
1042 LET S2=Y; S3=0
1045 REM -----------------------------------------------------------------
1051 IF C$="T" THEN 1088
1052 IF C$="S" THEN 1100
1070 PRINT#D, A, TAB(6), C$, TAB(8), T$, TAB(30), "$", B, TAB(40), "$", Y, TAB(50), "$", M
1078 REM -----------------------------------------------------------------
1080 PRINT "DO YOU HAVE MORE "; A; " ACCOUNTS TO ENTER ?"; INPUT Y$
1082 IF Y$="NO" THEN 1148
1084 IF Y$="YES" THEN 1120
1085 PRINT "CAN'T SPELL, HUH.. "
1086 GOTO 1080
1088 REM -------------------------------PRINT----------------------------
1089 PRINT#D
1090 PRINT#D, A, TAB(6), C$, TAB(8), T$
1091 GOTO 1148
1100 REM -------------------------------TOTAL----------------------------
1105 PRINT#D, A, TAB(6), C$, TAB(8), T$, TAB(30), "$", T1, TAB(40), "$", T2, TAB(50), "$", T3
1108 PRINT#2, A; C$; T$; "$"; T1; "$"; T2; "$"; T3
1110 IF W=1 THEN 1160
1115 LET W=1; E1=T1; E2=T2; E3=T3; T1=0; T2=0; T3=0
1118 GOTO 1035
1120 REM -----------------------------------------------------------------
1122 LET A1=A
1125 PRINT "ACCOUNT (3 DIGITS)     : "; A1
1126 PRINT "DATE (MM/DD)           : "; INPUT D$
1127 PRINT "CHECK NUMBER (3 DIG)   : "; INPUT K$
1128 PRINT "DESCRIPTION (20 CHAR): "; INPUT U$
1129 PRINT "AMOUNT                $"; INPUT M
1130 LET S2=S2+M; S3=S3+M
1140 PRINT#D, A1, TAB(8), D$, TAB(15), K$, TAB(20), U$, TAB(50), "$", M
1145 GOTO 1080
1148 REM ----------------UPDATE CHART OF ACCOUNTS------------------
1150 PRINT#2, A; C$; T$; "$"; B; "$"; S2; "$"; 0000.00
1151 IF C$#"+" THEN 1035
1152 PRINT#D, "-----------------------------------------------------------------"
1153 PRINT#D, A, TAB(6), C$, TAB(8), T$, TAB(30), "$", B, TAB(40), "$", S2, TAB(50), "$", S3
1154 PRINT#D
1155 LET T1=T1+B; T2=T2+S2; T3=T3+S3
1157 GOTO 1035
1158 REM ----------------------END OF LOOP---------------------------
1160 LET T1=E1-T1; T2=E2-T2; T3=E3-T3
1165 PRINT#D, TAB(10), "INCOME - EXPENSES  : ", TAB(30), "$", T1, TAB(40), "$", T2;
1166 PRINT#D, TAB(50), "$", T3
1168 REM -----------------------------------------------------------------
1170 END#1
1171 END#2
1172 END
```

Fig. 8.6 BASIC program for transaction processing

tion. This approach provides a back-up copy of the previous month's budget.

The program of Fig. 8.6 again uses sequential file access to read the chart-of-accounts file and write a new file. Lines 1030 and 1032 open these two (input and output) files under the names supplied by the user.

In lines 1040 and 1041, the program continues to read an item at a time from the input chart until the end-of-file mark is encountered. In line 1042, the year-to-date total is used to initialize the summation probe, S2. The probe S3 is reset to zero because it sums the monthly transactions only.

In lines 1051 and 1052, the program determines the type of processing to be done. If the account code is T, the title is not processed, but instead it is directly written to the output file. If the action code is S, then one of the two possible summation titles has been reached. In the case of an INCOME summation, the program checks W to note that the summation is in fact for INCOME (see line 1110). Line 1115 saves the INCOME sums and begins processing the EXPENSE portion with $T1$, $T2$, $T3$ set to zero.

In lines 1122 to 1129, the operator is lead through an input. Since the account number is already known from the chart account number, this is not requested ($A1 = A$). The year-to-date sum ($S2$) and monthly total ($S3$) are computed, and the transaction is then printed.

The transaction processing program is highly interactive and simple. It is *not*, however representative of the way many systems operate because most general ledger systems of the past were implemented on impersonal computers.

Report Generation

The Income Statement

The second time the transaction processing program of Fig. 8.6 was run, it produced the output of Fig. 8.7. In this report, notice the year-to-date column. The author is still being underpaid by his publisher, but notice that the year-to-date sum is $330, reflecting the carry forward from the past month.

Actually, this simple system combines the income statement with a balance sheet report. The balance of each item is printed immediately below the horizontal dotted line. The total INCOME minus EXPENSES account is provided at the end of the statement, as shown by the (loss) amount in Fig. 8.7.

```
CHART OF ACCOUNTS FOR FILE :      JULY
OUTPUT CHART OF ACCOUNTS FILE :  AUGUST
ACCT:CODE:      TITLE              BUDGET     YEAR-TO-DATE    CURRENT MO.

100   T       INCOME
101   + NET PAYCHECK            $   600    $      600$          0
101      08/01   97    TEACHING            $                  300
101      08/15   97    TEACHING            $                  300
----------------------------------------------------------------------------
101   + NET PAYCHECK            $   600    $     1200$         600

102   + PUBLISHERS ROYALTIES    $   250    $      230$          0
102      08/28   44    HAYDEN BOOKS        $                  100
----------------------------------------------------------------------------
102   + PUBLISHERS ROYALTIES    $   250    $      330$         100

199   S TOTAL  INCOME           $   850    $     1530$         700

200   T        EXPENSES
201   + FOOD                    $   200    $     172.54$        0
201      08/18   213   MARKETS             $                  129.55
----------------------------------------------------------------------------
201   + FOOD                    $   200    $     302.09$       129.55

202   + HOUSING                 $   275    $     380.85$        0
202      08/10   243   RENT&UTILITIES      $                  348.5
----------------------------------------------------------------------------
202   + HOUSING                 $   275    $     729.35$       348.5

300   + CLOTHING                $    85    $      48$           0
----------------------------------------------------------------------------
300   + CLOTHING                $    85    $      48$           0

400   + TRANSPORTATION          $    75    $     125$           0
400      08/23   256   CAR PAYMT           $                  125
400      08/19   201   GAS CREDIT CD       $                  143.39
----------------------------------------------------------------------------
400   + TRANSPORTATION          $    75    $     393.39$       268.39

500   + PERSONAL                $    55    $      0$            0
----------------------------------------------------------------------------
500   + PERSONAL                $    55    $      0$            0

600   + EDUCATION               $    25    $      0$            0
----------------------------------------------------------------------------
600   + EDUCATION               $    25    $      0$            0

601   + RECREATION              $    60    $      0$            0
----------------------------------------------------------------------------
601   + RECREATION              $    60    $      0$            0

701   + MEDICAL                 $    20    $      0$            0
701      08/12   233   CHECK-UP            $                   35
----------------------------------------------------------------------------
701   + MEDICAL                 $    20    $      35$          35

801   + SAVINGS                 $    25    $      35$           0
----------------------------------------------------------------------------
801   + SAVINGS                 $    25    $      35$           0

900   + MISCELLANEOUS           $    30    $      15$           0
----------------------------------------------------------------------------
900   + MISCELLANEOUS           $    30    $      15$           0

999   S TOTAL   EXPENSES        $   850    $     1557.83$      781.44
         INCOME - EXPENSES      $     0    $     -27.8301$     -81.4401
```

Fig. 8.7 Second run of transaction processing for Lewis

Additional Comments

We pointed out several discrepancies between the system Arnold invented and typical general ledger systems of the past. Of course, Arnold devised a system for his personal use rather than one for his business. But what are the differences?

A general ledger system typically consists of a chart-of-accounts file similar to Arnold's. It consists of a transaction file that is separately maintained and stored during the month. At the end of the month, the transaction file is sorted to bring together all transactions with identical account numbers and to prepare the transaction file for merging with the chart-of-accounts file.

A trial balance is computed rather than an income statement, as shown in Fig. 8.7. The trial balance is inspected to make sure debits equal credits. Once the trial balance is obtained, a balance sheet consisting of a summary is printed. This table of year-to-date balances is then recorded by updating the chart-of-accounts file.

The two-file system has advantages over Arnold's system. The trial balance gives an additional audit check before changes to the chart are allowed. It also allows input of transactions in any order.

Arnold's system can be enhanced by adding other subprograms. For example, a subprogram to modify, insert, or delete chart-of-account titles, balances, and numbers would be useful. A similar subprogram for the transaction file would be valuable.

By the way, although Arnold's Peace Plan I worked fine, it ended up in an unexpected way. First, Arnold became addicted to the kids' personal computer and stopped watching TV every night. His wife had a baby girl, but a few years later she ran off with an insurance salesman. Arnold found out about it several months after she left and filed for divorce.

The two boys, Adolph and Albert, complained to their father about not getting enough time on what they regarded as their personal computer. Finally Arnold broke down and loaned them enough money to open a computer shop near the Royal Hawaiian Hotel on Waikiki. Since Arnold contents himself now just doing their taxes, he knows how well they are doing.

Chapter Nine

TWENTY-FIRST CENTURY REAL ESTATE

GRADUATION DAY: *A man and his son were about to part, perhaps forever. The milestone was a profound event for them both.*

"I have remembered the lessons you taught me, father," said the young son.

"I hope they serve you well, son," the father replied, trying to be the stronger of the two. "But there is one more thing I must tell you before you go."

"What is that, father?"

The father paused to find the right words for what he wanted to say. "Most of the things I told you are true, son."

"Yes, father." The boy-man looked up.

"I only lied when I had to, son, and that was mostly concerning little things."

"Oh," said the son.

Merlin L. Sales grew up in Boston. He knew every street, building, alley, and trash can in downtown Boston. When he was 14 years old, he delivered groceries to the inhabitants of the Lithuanian section of the city for his father. Later he drove a taxi to support himself while attending Boston College. In short, he knew Boston real estate.

When Merlin finished his business degree, the first and only job he considered was buying and selling real estate. Like many other systems studied in this book, the success of Merlin's business led him to turn to computing as a means of coping with paperwork.

In the following case study, we examine techniques for storing and retrieving data that are described by nonunique keys. This kind of database, called an *attribute-based database*, differs from the previous systems discussed in this book because of the nonuniqueness of access keys. This feature of the real estate retrieval problem is a common feature of many useful database systems.

While the techniques to follow are sophisticated and often difficult to understand, they are extremely useful. The extra effort and time required to understand the techniques to follow are well worth it.

The Multiple Listing Problem

Merlin L. Sales runs a real estate office called Twenty-First Century Real Estate that handles over a thousand property listings each week. His salespeople are limited only by their ability to match a client's request with the listings currently for sale. Given a general description of the desired property, the salesperson looks through a file containing descriptions and pictures of those for sale. When a collection of properties are found that might be of interest to the client, the salesperson and client visit the site to examine it further.

Merlin is painfully aware of the fact that most of the time in selling is spent on "false drops," that is, showing clients property in which they are not interested. Furthermore, the clerical staff at Twenty-First Century Real Estate spend many hours each day searching their MLS (multiple-listing-service) files for matching properties. What Merlin needs is a fast retrieval system that can yield information on property that will match the requests of individual clients.

The For-Sale File

The MLS for-sale file contains descriptions of every home on the Boston market. This file is kept up-to-date by adding new listings as they become available. It is maintained manually, however, and sometimes the information it contains is several days out-of-date. On several occasions, Merlin's salespeople have lost a sale because their for-sale file was obsolete.

The for-sale file, or MLS file as it will be called here, is a collection of records that describe the attributes of a house. Through the years, Merlin has learned that buyers are most interested in the items illustrated in Fig. 9.1. The records of Fig. 9.1 are stored in the MLS for-sale file.

Actually, most clients are concerned with only a very few features of a house when first looking at a property. The details of Fig. 9.1 are less interesting to a buyer at that time. Merlin has observed this phenomenon and organized the MLS file around a small collection of attributes.

Attributes of Property

The three most important attributes of the properties listed in Fig. 9.1 are shown in Fig. 9.2 in a multiple-choice format. In Fig. 9.2(B), the parenthesized numbers indicate the attributes of cost, location, and number of bedrooms. These numbers are keyed to the multiple-choice list of Fig. 9.2(A). For example, (3, 2, 2) refers to all houses with three bedrooms, located on the other side of town, and priced

MLS NUMBER	:	945
ASKING PRICE	:	$38,595
LOCATION	:	15938 SW Truman Rd.
NUMBER BEDROOMS	:	THREE
NUMBER BATHS	:	1½
SALES STATUS	:	EARNEST MONEY
COMMENTS	:	CORNER LOT WITH TREES
MLS NUMBER	:	328
ASKING PRICE	:	$49,995
LOCATION	:	1825 Oak Blvd.
NUMBER BEDROOMS	:	FOUR
NUMBER BATHS	:	3
SALES STATUS	:	SOLD
COMMENTS	:	FINANCING AVAILABLE
MLS NUMBER	:	1109
ASKING PRICE	:	$29,800
LOCATION	:	5220 Railroad St.
NUMBER BEDROOMS	:	TWO
NUMBER BATHS	:	2
SALES STATUS	:	FORSALE
COMMENTS	:	UNFINISHED FAMILY ROOM

Fig. 9.1 Sample properties from the MLS for-sale file

(A) The Attribute List

COST
1. $10,000–19,999
2. $20,000–29,999
3. $30,000–39,999
4. Greater than $40,000

LOCATION
1. This side of town
2. The other side of town

NUMBER OF BEDROOMS
1. Two
2. Three
3. Four or more

(B) The Attributes of Fig. 9.1 Property

MLS #945 = (3, 2, 2)
MLS #328 = (4, 1, 3)
MLS #1109 = (2, 2, 1)

Fig. 9.2 The attributes of MLS property

at \$30,000 to \$39,999. It happens that MLS #945 matches this set of attributes. It may also be possible for another property to match the set of three numbers. This is why any such triplet must be considered a nonunique key.

Merlin marks each property description with a triplet of this sort and files it in a cabinet with other descriptions bearing the same triplet so that properties of similar features may be easily accessed. Unfortunately, the retrieval speed of Merlin's attribute-based filing system is too slow.

Where Is Invention When You Need It?

Merlin L. Sales and associates wasted no time in purchasing a small computer to solve their retrieval problem. The trouble began in earnest when they learned that the computer they owned was unable to retrieve information stored by the attribute-based file method which they had been using for years. Here is what happened.

The first approach tried by Merlin and his hired programmer worked on a sequential file of properties stored by MLS number. The MLS number being used as a key, each record was retrieved, compared, and either discarded or else printed when a match occurred. This method also proved too slow for Merlin and his impatient clients.

The second method used index files. An index subfile was established for each attribute. The COST subfile contained the price of each property listed in the MLS file; the LOCATION subfile stored location information; and the BEDROOM subfile stored the number of bedrooms. First, the retrieval system would access only those records that matched the number of bedrooms. Then, the records that satisfied the number of bedrooms requested but failed to satisfy the other two attributes were discarded. The remaining records were printed to indicate their sales status.

This method was faster but still too slow. Furthermore, Merlin rejected it because it required three times as much storage as the sequential file. The subfiles were very space-consuming and left little room for the MLS file.

Advanced File Structuring

Searching and the Woe It Brings

Merlin discovered that computers are very slow if they are not properly programmed. He temporarily gave up his project of computerizing the MLS file because it "ain't yet practical." He and his associates returned to the old hand method.

Several months later Merlin learned that his golf partner Joe had a brilliant son in high school who owned his own computer. Merlin told Joe of his failure and said that Joe's kid could come by and use his computer because it was useless to him.

The next day Joe's son Marion stopped in to visit the real estate office, and by the end of the day, Marion had solved Merlin's problem. His MLS attribute file program was fast and compact. How did Marion do it?

Is Hashing Legal?

We discussed the concept of hashing in the previous chapter. Now we are faced with a problem that requires it because every other approach fails as a result of speed or memory restrictions.

Recall that a key is hashed by computing a quotient and remainder by dividing the key by a prime number equal to the size of the file. The remainder is used as the random (direct) access number unless the direct access leads to a collision with another record. In a collision, the remainder is offset by adding the quotient to it and trying a subsequent direct access with the new value for record number. We continue to add the quotient in order to access a record that has not been allocated.

The process is repeated to find a record, given its key, when we want to perform a look-up. This idea is very important to the method, because it means that we can use the same program to look up, insert, or delete a record in a random access file merely by giving the program a single key.

The hashing routine used by Joe's son is shown in Fig. 9.3. The key for multiple attributes (cost, location, bedrooms) is computed as I1 in these programs. In the next section, we will discover why I1 is useful in helping to select the correct MLS record from all other records.

The hashing algorithm of Fig. 9.3 works on arrays I, F, and K. These arrays are stored in main memory in this example, but they would be a subfile in a larger database. In either case, they comprise what is called a *directory.*

The value of F1 determines what action is to be performed by the hashing routine.

If F1 = (−1), the routine will perform either a look-up or delete when the key-to-record number access finds an "empty" record in the file. This is signified by F(R) = NONE in the blueprints. If F1 = (+1), the routine returns the location of an available record so that additions may be inserted here.

(A) BLUE₀

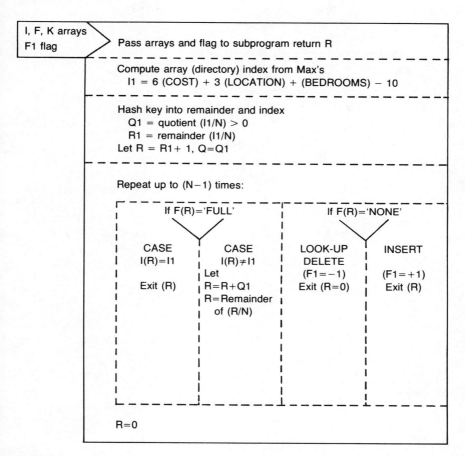

(B) BLUE₁

1. PROGRAM: Search the Directory

2. DATA:
    - I1 = index, initially computed
    - Q1 = quotient, computed > 0
    - R1 = remainder, computed
    - Q = temporary quotient, computed
    - R = temporary remainder, computed
    - N = length of directory arrays, initially passed
    - F1 = action code, (−1) for look-up, (+1) for inserting additions, initially passed
    - F = array of flag values, either (−1) if "none" or (+1) if "full," initially (−1)
    - I = array of index values, initially zero

Fig. 9.3 Directory search subprogram

3. STEPS:
    3.1. Compute:

$$I1 = 6 \cdot C + 3 \cdot L + B - 10$$
$$Q1 = \text{INT } (I1/N); \; R1 = I1 - Q \cdot N$$
$$Q1 = 1$$

            If Q1>0 then skip "over"
     over: R   = R1+1; Q = Q1

    3.2. Repeat up to (N−1) times:
          3.2.1 If F(R)>0 then skip to 3.2.2
                If F1>0 then skip to "exit"
                R = 0
                Goto "exit"
          3.2.2 If I(R) = I1 then "exit"
                Try again: R = R + Q1
                            Q = INT(R/N)
                            R1 = INT(R−Q·N)
                            R = R1 + 2
                            Goto end of loop
    3.3. R = 0 (no match)
    3.4. "exit": Return R

(C) BLUE₂

```
5000 REM *********************************************************************
5001 REM                    HASHED-ARRAY SEARCH SUBPROGRAM
5002 REM                         COPYRIGHT 1977
5003 REM *********************************************************************
5010 LET I1=6*C+3*L+B-10
5020 LET Q1=INT(I1/N); R1=INT(I1-Q1*N)
5030 IF Q1>0 THEN 5050
5040 LET Q1=1
5050 LET R=R1+1; Q=Q1
5060 REM *****************REPEAT*********************************************
5070 FOR J=1 TO(N-1)
5075 IF F[R]>0 THEN 5100
5080 IF F1>0 THEN 5500
5090 LET R=0
5095 GOTO 5500
5100 REM ----------------3.2.2----------------------------------------------
5105 IF I[R]=I1 THEN 5500
5110 LET R=R+Q1; Q=INT(R/N); R1=INT(R-Q*N); R=R1+1
5200 NEXT J
5300 REM ----------------END LOOP-------------------------------------------
5310 LET R=0
5500 RETURN
```

Fig. 9.3 Continued

The Attribute File

    In order to understand fully the clever method invented by Joe's brilliant son we need to study an example. The attribute file of Fig. 9.4 illustrates how a linked list structure is combined with the directory to accomplish the fast look-up and economy of storage that Merlin was looking for. The arrays F, I, and K are shown as a single directory.

    The attribute file operates as follows. The triplet (cost, location, bedrooms) is used to compute a value for I. This value is computed from a formula that is shown in Fig. 9.3(A):

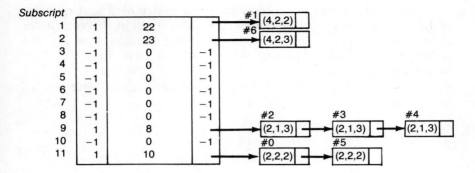

Insertions in this order:
      (2,2,2) → Record #0
      (4,2,2) → Record #1
      (2,1,3) → Record #2
      (2,1,3) → Record #3
      (2,1,3) → Record #4
      (2,2,2) → Record #5
      (4,2,3) → Record #6

Fig. 9.4 The MLS attribute file

$$I1 = 6(COST) + 3(LOCATION) + (BEDROOMS) - 10$$

In general, we can compute I1 from the formula,

$$I1 = \left(\sum_{S=1}^{n-1} (\overset{r=S}{\pi} Maximum_{r+1})(I_S - 1) \right) + (I_n - 1)$$

where

$$Maximum_r = \text{rth subscript maximum value}$$
$$I_S = \text{Sth subscript in triplet } (I_1, \dots I_S, \dots I_n)$$

In Fig. 9.4, the Maximum$_r$ values are 4, 2, 3, respectively. The values of I_S are shown for each record inserted into the file.

As a final check on understanding, we will work out an example using the data of Fig. 9.4. Suppose the user wishes to retrieve information about the type of house described below:

$10,000–19,999(1)
The other side of town(2)
Two bedrooms(1)

This selection yields the triplet (1, 2, 1). If we use the formula of Fig. 9.3(A) for I1, we get the value to be hashed into the directory.

$$I1 = 6(1) + 3(2) + (1) - 10 = 3$$

The hashing function produces a remainder of 3 and quotient of 1 (since $Q = 0$, it is incremented to 1). The result of this remainder is to search location 4 in the directory. Since location 4 in Fig. 9.4 is "empty," the look-up produces "NO HOUSES OF THAT KIND" as output.

Suppose the user wants information about the following type of house:

$20,000–29,999(2)
This side of town(1)
4 or more bedrooms(3)

In this case, the triplet (2, 1, 3) yields the following value for I1:

$$I1 = 6(2) + 3(1) + (3) - 10 = 8$$

The remainder is thus 8, and the quotient is 0 upon division by 11. The search produces three records beginning at location 9 of the directory.

The three arrays of Fig. 9.4 now have obvious meaning. The value of F indicates whether a directory "cell" is occupied (1) or empty (-1). The value stored in I is the number computed for I1 when the record is inserted into the file. This number is compared during a look-up to make sure that we have accessed the correct attribute. Without the value of I, we might confuse the possible synonyms resulting from a collision.

The value of K is the record number of the first record in the chain of similar houses. Initially, K is a negative number to indicate that no records are stored corresponding to the directory entry.

The MLS Database System

The MLS database runs fast because hashing provides a means of directly accessing all records of a given triplet of attributes. Once the chain of similar properties is located through the directory, the remaining records are accessed with a single direct access read. The advantages of this speed are evident.

The hashing scheme also allows a small memory overhead because the directory is much smaller than an index subfile. In most cases, the directory can be stored in main memory for speed, but even if the available space does not permit such storage, only a few additional accesses are required.

The directory should always contain empty space in order to keep the system running fast. It is known, for example, that the number of accesses needed to find an item in the directory can be computed by the following equation:

Number of accesses = $1/(1 - \text{Loading fraction})$

where the "loading fraction" is the fractional portion of directory actually used:

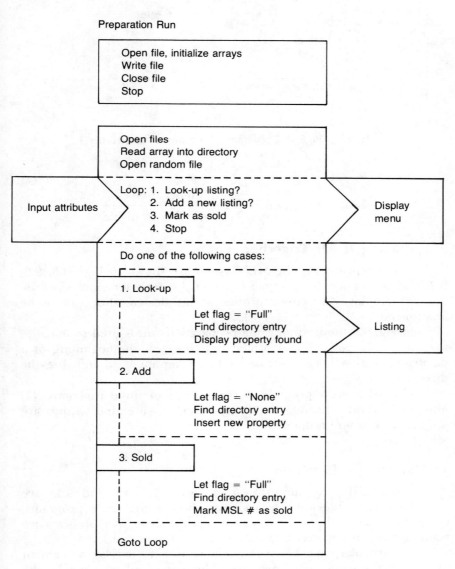

Fig. 9.5 Blueprint for MLS retrieval system

```
10 REM  ************************************************************
11 REM                REAL ESTATE SYSTEM
12 REM                    COPYRIGHT 1977
13 REM  ************************************************************
15 DIM F$[8], E$[8], F[50], I[50], K[50]
20 PRINT#D, "CENTURY 21 REAL ESTATE SYSTEM"
25 PRINT#D, "PASSWORD : "; INPUT F$
30 PRINT#D, "NAME OF MLS FILE : "; INPUT E$
35 REM -----------------------------------------------------------
40 OPEN#1, F$
50 PRINT#1, E$
60 PRINT#D, "INPUT SIZE OF DIRECTORY : "; INPUT N
65 LET W=0
69 REM -----------------------------------------------------------
70 PRINT#1, N; "#"; 000
80 FOR J=1 TO N
90 LET F[J]=(-1); I[J]=0; K[J]=(-1)
100 PRINT#1, F[J]; "F"; I[J]; "I"; K[J]
110 NEXT J
115 END#1
119 REM -----------------------------------------------------------
120 PRINT#D, "MLS DATABASE PREPARED"
130 APP "MLS"
```

Fig. 9.6 The BASIC program for preparation of MLS file

$$\text{Loading fraction} = \frac{\text{Number used}}{\text{Total number available}}$$

Putting It All Together

The blueprints for the MLS system are shown in Figs. 9.5, 9.6, 9.7, and 9.8. They are programs written by Joe's son, and since he did not employ correctness probes in his design, they cannot be guaranteed.

In Fig. 9.5, notice that a file preparation run is used to initialize the file. Initialization is performed only once, at the beginning of a database creation. The purpose of this program is to initialize the directory.

The MLS main program performs one of three functions: (1) look-up, (2) add a listing, or (3) sell a listing. All extinct listings are purged by a program not shown.

The Basic Routines

The BASIC programs shown in Figs. 9.9, 9.10, and 9.11 are self-explanatory. We must be cautious about using these programs, however, because there is no way to certify them. No probes have been inserted into the code to indicate correct operation.

In particular, the APP command is used to overlay a segment of the program into main memory. This command may not be the same on all versions of BASIC.

1. PROGRAM: MLS Subsystem Program

2. DATA:

    N   = length of array directory input
    F1 = action code for search subprogram, computed
    F   = array directory flag, input
    I   = array directory index, input
    K   = array director, pointer, input
    K1 = temporary record pointer for random access, computed
    M$ = MLS #, input
    C$ = cost, input
    C   = cost attribute, computed
    L$ = location, input
    L   = location attribute, computed
    B$ = number of bedrooms, input
    B   = number of bedrooms attribute, computed
    A$ = number of bathrooms, input
    S$ = status, sold, earnest money, or available, input
    Z$ = comments, input
    N1 = next-record-pointer, computed
    N$ = input value of MLS # for query, initially input
    V1 = random file record number of last write, initially input
    Y$ = filler string of length equal to combined lengths of the strings M$, C$, L$, B$,
            A$, S$, Z$, initially unknown
    GOSUB 2000 = print MLS listing
    GOSUB 5000 = search directory
    GOSUB 6000 = input attributes
    GOSUB 7000 = input full MLS descriptions

3. STEPS:

    3.1 Open preparation file, initialize arrays F, I, and K
        Close preparation file
        Open random file #1
    3.2 "Loop": Display menu of actions:
              Print
                 "1. Look-up MLS property
                 2. Add an MLS property
                 3. Sell an MLS property
                 4. Stop."
    3.3 Do only one of the following cases:
        3.3.1 *Look-up:* Get attributes: C, L, B (subprogram call)
                      Set flag F1 = (−1) for search on Full
                      Call search subprogram to get R
                      If R=0 then "Property Not Found"
                      Repeat until N1≤0: K1=K(R)
                        Input #1, M$; C$; L$; B$; A$; S$; Z$, N1 (from K1)
                        Print #D, M$, C$, L$, B$, A$, S$, Z$
                        Let K1=N1
                      Goto "Loop"
        3.3.2 *Add:*   Get attributes: C, L, B (call subprogram)
                      Get descriptions: M$, C$, L$, B$, A$, S$, Z$
                      Set flag F1 = 1

Fig. 9.7   Blueprints for MLS retrieval subsystem

Call search subprogram to get R
If R=0 then "Directory Full"
Increment V1 = V1 + 1
Print #1, M$; C$; L$; B$; A$; S$; Z$;
    I1 into record V1
If I(R) = I1 then skip to "chain"
Update: K(R) = V1
         I(R) = I1
         F(R) = 1
Goto "Loop"

"Chain": Input #1, Y$, N1 from record K(R)
If N1≤0 then set N1=V1
     Print #1, Y$; N1
     Goto "Loop"

"Directory Full": Print #D, "Directory Full, Reorganize"
Goto "Loop"

3.3.3 *Sold:*   Get Attributes: C, L, B
Get ML$#, input #D, N$
Set flag F1=(−1)
Call search program to get R
If R=0 then "Property Not Found"
Repeat until N1=0: K1=K(R), initially
    Input #1, M$; C$; L$; B$, A$, S$; Z$; N1 from K1
If M$ = N$ then skip to "Sellit"
Let K1 = N1
Goto "Loop"

"sellit": Print #1, M$, C$, L$; B$; A$;
    "SOLD"; Z$; N1 into K1
Goto "Loop"

3.4 Stop (999)

Fig. 9.7 Continued

```
5 LET D=0
10 REM ************************************************************
11 REM          MLS SUBSYSTEM
12 REM          COPYRIGHT 1977
13 REM ************************************************************
15 DIM F$[8], E$[8], F[50], I[50], K[50], G$[8], X$[1]
18 DIM M$[5], C$[6], L$[20], B$[10], A$[10], S$[5], Z$[20], N$[5], Y$[76]
20 PRINT#D, "CENTURY 21 REAL ESTATE SYSTEM"
25 PRINT#D, "PASSWORD   : "; INPUT F$
30 PRINT#D, "NAME OF MLS FILE : "; INPUT E$
40 OPEN#1, F$
50 INPUT#1, G$
60 IF G$=E$ THEN 90
70 PRINT#D, "IMPROPER ACCESS, TRY AGAIN"
80 GOTO 20
90 INPUT#1, N; X$; V1
100 FOR J=1 TO N
110 INPUT#1, F[J]; X$; I[J]; X$; K[J]
115 NEXT J
120 END#1
130 OPEN#1, E$
135 REM -----------------------------LOOP-----------------------------
140 PRINT#D, "SELECT ONE OF THE FOLLOWING : "
141 PRINT#D, "1. LOOK-UP MLS PROPERTY"
```

Fig. 9.8 The BASIC main program for MLS

```
142 PRINT#D, "2. ADD AN MLS PROPERTY "
143 PRINT#D, "3. SELL AN MLS PROPERTY"
144 PRINT#D, "4. STOP"
145 PRINT#D, "ENTER 1, 2, 3, OR 4 :"; INPUT C
146 IF C=4 THEN 999
147 IF C=3 THEN 300
148 IF C=2 THEN 200
149 IF C#1 THEN 140
150 REM -------------------DO ONE OF THESE----------------------------
151 REM ------LOOK-UP--------------------------------------------------
155 GOSUB 6000
160 LET F1=(-1)
165 GOSUB 5000
170 IF R#0 THEN 180
174 PRINT#D, "PROPERTY NOT FOUND"
176 GOTO 140
178 REM -----------REPEAT UNTIL N1<0 ------------------------------
179 LET K1=K[R]
180 RESTORE#1, K1
182 INPUT#1, M$; C$; L$; B$; A$; S$; Z$; N1
184 GOSUB 2000
186 LET K1=N1
188 IF K1<0 THEN 140; GOTO 180
189 REM ----------ADD A PROPERTY ------------------------------
200 GOSUB 6000
210 GOSUB 7000
212 LET F1=1
215 GOSUB 5000
220 IF R=0 THEN 275
222 REM ------------------------------------------------------------
225 LET V1=V1+1; RESTORE#1, V1
230 PRINT#1, M$; C$; L$; B$; A$; S$; Z$; (-1)
235 IF I[R]=I1 THEN 250
240 LET K[R]=V1; I[R]=I1; F[R]=1
245 GOTO 140
249 REM ---------------------CHAIN--------------------------
250 RESTORE#1, K[R]
253 INPUT#1, Y$; N1
255 IF N1>=0 THEN 140
260 LET N1=V1; RESTORE#1, K[R]
265 PRINT#1, Y$; N1
270 GOTO 140
274 REM ------------------DIRECTORY FULL---------------------
275 PRINT#D, "DIRECTORY FULL...REORGANIZE"
280 GOTO 140
288 REM ----------------------SOLD---------------------------
300 GOSUB 6000
310 PRINT#D, "INPUT MLS# :"; INPUT N$
320 LET F1=(-1)
325 GOSUB 5000
330 IF R=0 THEN 174
331 REM ----------------REPEAT UNTIL N1<0 --------------------
335 LET K1=K[R]
340 RESTORE#1, K1
345 INPUT#1, M$; C$; L$; B$; A$; S$; Z$; N1
350 IF M$=N$ THEN 380
355 LET K1=N1
360 IF K1<0 THEN 140; GOTO 340
370 REM ------------------------SELL IT ---------------------------
375 RESTORE#1, K1
380 PRINT#1, M$; C$; L$; B$; A$; " SOLD"; Z$; N1
390 GOTO 140
400 REM ------------------------------------------------------------
999 END#1
1000 OPEN#1, F$
1010 PRINT#1, N, "#"; V1
1020 FOR J=1 TO N
1025 PRINT#1, F[J]; "F"; I[J]; "I"; K[J]
1028 NEXT J
1030 END#1
1035 PRINT#D, "MLS SYSTEM ENDED"
1040 STOP
```

Fig. 9.8 Continued

```
2000 REM ********************
2001 REM    PRINT MLS LIST
2002 REM ********************
2010 PRINT#D, "MLS PROPERTY : ", M$
2020 PRINT#D, TAB(10), "PRICE        $", C$
2030 PRINT#D, TAB(10), "LOCATION     : ", L$
2040 PRINT#D, TAB(10), "#BEDROOMS    : ", B$, " AND BATHS : ", A$
2050 PRINT#D, TAB(10), "SALES STATUS : ", S$
2060 PRINT#D, TAB(5), "COMMENTS : ", Z$
2070 REM ------------------------
2080 RETURN
```

Fig. 9.9   BASIC subroutine for printing MLS records

```
6000 REM *************************
6001 REM    INPUT ATTRIBUTES
6002 REM *************************
6010 PRINT#D, "ASKING PRICE : "
6020 PRINT#D, TAB(10), "1. $10,000 - 19,999"
6030 PRINT#D, TAB(10), "2. $20,000 - 29,999"
6040 PRINT#D, TAB(10), "3. $30,000 - 39,999"
6050 PRINT#D, TAB(10), "4. MORE THAN $40,000"
6060 PRINT#D, "ENTER 1,2,3 OR 4 : "; INPUT C
6110 REM
6120 PRINT#D, "LOCATION : "
6130 PRINT#D, TAB(10), "1. THIS SIDE OF TRACKS"
6140 PRINT#D, TAB(10), "2. THAT SIDE OF TRACKS"
6150 PRINT#D, "ENTER 1 OR 2 : "; INPUT L
6160 REM
6210 PRINT#D, "HOW MANY BEDROOMS : "
6220 PRINT#D, TAB(10), "1. 2 BEDROOMS"
6230 PRINT#D, TAB(10), "2. 3 BEDROOMS"
6240 PRINT#D, TAB(10), "3. 4 OR MORE  "
6250 PRINT#D, "ENTER 1,2 OR 3 : "; INPUT B
6260 REM
6300 RETURN
```

Fig. 9.10   BASIC subprogram for inputting attributes

```
7000 REM **************************
7001 REM    INPUT MLS RECORDS
7002 REM **************************
7010 PRINT#D, "MLS PROPERTY DETAILS"
7020 PRINT#D, "MLS NUMBER       : "; INPUT M$
7025 PRINT#D, "ASKING PRICE    $"; INPUT C$
7030 PRINT#D, "LOCATION         : "; INPUT L$
7035 PRINT#D, "NUMBER BEDROOMS  : "; INPUT B$
7040 PRINT#D, "NUMBER BATHS     : "; INPUT A$
7045 PRINT#D, "SALES STATUS     : "; INPUT S$
7050 PRINT#D, "COMMENTS         : "; INPUT Z$
7060 REM
7080 RETURN
```

Fig. 9.11   BASIC subprogram for inputting full MLS records

Chapter Ten

How to Profit from the Coming

Revolution

"U av it gud, my son," the 120-year-old man said to his 35-year-old son. "Wy, wen I wuz 35 years old, pepol killed each other by driving their cars to their werk stations inside big bildings."

"Wy did thay do such stoopid things, fawther?" the younger man replied. "It seems lyk such a wayst of time and munee."

The two men were sitting at home, one in New York, the other in Phoenix. The living room of each contained a laser projection system that created a three-dimensional image of the other as they sat chatting. The father appeared to sit next to his son in Phoenix, while, simultaneously, the son appeared to be sitting across from his father in New York.

"It's a long story, son, but I must go to werk, myself, now. We can tawk more later." The father smiled and turned to insert a cassette tape into a video reader. The tape contained a program that dialed his office and set up a holographic image of it and two of his co-workers on a screen. The screen also displayed a list of reminders.

One of the workers turned around and said, "Gud morning, sir, we av sum items to discus with U."

Both workers were actually located in different villages as well. Their images were being superimposed onto the image of an office that did not exist. It was merely a simulation to create the psychological feeling of work.

A window to the future, 1994

Computers Are Free, but Peripherals Ain't

The basic thesis of this book is the idea that computers are free, or affordable by everyone. Actually, of course, this is not yet a reality. The reasons for falling short of a computer utopia where anyone can afford an impressive computer system have been glossed over in the preceding chapters. We should be able to discover these reasons, now, with hindsight.

159

Once he understands where improvements are needed, the futurologist can make predictions about what will happen when the problems are solved. These predictions will be most useful in writing a scenario of the future. For the reader with a profit motive, the ability to tell the future can be very useful, indeed.

We will not guarantee that all the problems and solutions proposed here will in fact become a reality. Furthermore, if they do become realities, we cannot say for sure when they will do so. All that can be claimed is that there are some things that are *probable,* this claim being based on events that have taken place in the past.

The predictions offered here for entertainment are based on the following past experiences.

1. *Profit:* The advancement of technology is governed by an expanding dollar volume market.

2. *Thresholds:* The popularity and success of a product depends upon its ability to break through various thresholds that exist at various points in time.

3. *Cost threshold:* There is a certain maximum cost, that whenever a product becomes available at or below this cost, it becomes a common commercial or business purchase. Similarly, there is a certain minimum cost at which a purchase will be made regardless of further decreases in price. (An example of the last maxim is demonstrated by the success of pocket calculators. The maximum cost appears to be several hundred dollars, while the minimum cost is tens of dollars. The market is not stimulated further by lowering the price below $10.)

4. *Utility threshold:* There is a certain minimum utility that must be real or imagined by consumers before a product is purchased. (The public must be convinced that they need TV games or personal computers because of their utility, e.g., status, comfort, increased competition, amusement. Without this increased utility provided by the technological gadget, it will never become a commercial or business product. We will appraise the new memory technologies possible in our future by studying their utility.)

5. *Survival:* There are some technological advances that must become a reality for mankind to survive. These gadgets provide energy, food, population control, and the like.

Since the needs and desires of a nation are less meaningful in the abstract, we shall pose scenarios for Jack Sharpe, a hypothetical man of the future, and Julie Zowie, a hypothetical woman of the future. Assuming that these two people are subject to the five motivations for future development, what is in store for them and their personal computers?

New Memories for the Future

Clearly, one of the biggest problems encountered in personal computing is the need for low-cost mass storage. Files were used to store large programs and data in the examples previously studied. These files posed a level of complication we would have preferred to avoid. How will the system of the future overcome this problem?

Jack Sharpe lives in a village yet to be on an island called Niu located in the South Pacific between Tonga and Cook Islands. He is employed by a sea farm corporation dealing in food, minerals, and energy derived from the ocean.

Jack is considering the floor plans of a new underwater home to be built for his family of four. The plans show a central computer system that will combine control of his home with the data processing needs of his office. Jack requested the system so that he will be able to spend more time at home with his family (utility) and keep up with his duties as oceanographer for the sea farm (survival, profit). The problem at hand is estimating the data storage capacity that his system will require to keep all the data he needs at his fingertips.

The office system that Jack envisions is a collection of facilities as shown in Fig. 10.1. The heart of Jack's system is a personal computer having the size of a 1977 model personal computer, but with ten times the speed and capacity of the outdated systems of the seventies.

The underwater building for Jack's family and office system is controlled by a "process control" capability. In addition, the process

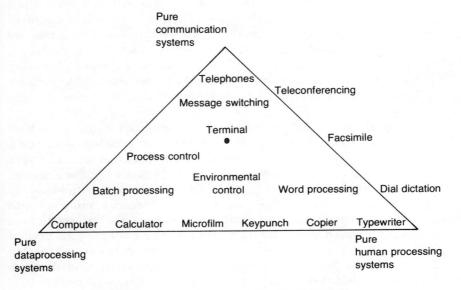

Fig. 10.1 The business system of Jack Sharpe

control subsystem allows Jack to monitor his sea garden from a robot submarine. The terminal located in Jack's study also monitors all telephone calls, and when Jack is not at home, the calls are answered with a voice response subsystem that responds with a different prerecorded message for every different voice pattern it detects.

Jack holds most of his meetings by teleconferencing with the corporate headquarters people in Los Angeles, New York, and Paris. His personal computer takes care of dialing and setting up all calls. His facsimile subsystem handles copies of diagrams, pictures, and necessary graphics.

Jack has no need for keypunching, calculators, batch processing, or typewriters, but his system has access to all of them if he later decides that they are necessary.

The business system of Fig. 10.1 requires an enormous amount of processing speed and storage capacity. Even by the eighties, the speed problem will be solved by microcomputers capable of billions of calculations per second. In addition, the system of Fig. 10.1 actually includes hundreds of microprocessors, each dedicated to special functions and each operating simultaneously.

The new memory technology needed by Jack actually consists of a variety of devices, each serving a different purpose. For example, the main memory is an LSI device capable of storing 64KB characters for each of the 812 microcomputers in the system. Thus, the combined main memory of Jack's system is 51.9MB (mega bytes). But even this is not enough for the business of the future.

A rotating magnetic bubble memory is thus included in the word processing subsystem of Jack's office. The tiny magnetic domains of this system move over an obstacle course at high speed in a manner analogous to that of rotating disk memories. Each 10MB module is the size of a pocket calculator and is inserted into the word processing system when its information is needed. Jack uses the bubble memory to help him with legal questions, making contracts, and retrieving past sales records.

The third level of memory required in Jack's system is *archival storage.* Jack has millions of files that are only occasionally needed. These files never change, but they do contain data that would be very expensive to get any other way except from archival storage. For example, the encyclopedia used by his two children is stored in holographic plastic sheets. These are inserted into a laser reader and read into his personal computer. The computer processes the information to extract only that desired and then prints it. The last time Jack needed archival storage was to retrieve sales records from ten years ago. He had to make a presentation to corporate headquarters, and the sales data were included on a graph sent to his superiors by facsimile.

Jack Sharpe completed his home/office in the sea and moved his family there. The house is his office, home, and recreation center for months at a time. It is truly a push-button home.

Push-Button Programming

The personal computer in Jack's vision of the perfect home would never have been possible if BASIC programs controlled the entire system. The personal computer of the future is a push-button computer. It is as simple to operate as a pocket calculator, but of course there are many more buttons to be pushed.

Jack has three stations in his home/office. The bedroom and study stations are for work, while the living room station is used for amusement. The work stations have a CRT and keyboard, but that is where similarity with the personal computers of the seventies ends. (The living room station is combined with the TV and stereo system). The keyboard is variable, which means that active keys light up while inactive keys remain dark. When a key is green, the user may push it. When a key is red, the user *must* push it. The numbers, letters, and words on each key change with the function to be performed.

In addition, the stations are equipped with voice response units to provide music, speech, and telephone conversations. The units are coordinated with the keyboard and CRT.

Jack uses the system by entering prerecorded commands or by pushing predefined buttons. If he wants to access information stored in a relational file, he enters the commands:

GIVE ME SALES-DATA FOR 1984
SORT SALES-DATA INTO ASCENDING ORDER
DISPLAY SALES-DATA ONTO SCREEN AND PRINTER
REPLACE MONTH-OF-AUGUST WITH NEW-MONTH
SAVE SALES-DATA

When ready to visit a friend by the name of George in Atlanta and another by the name of Jon in Las Vegas, Jack enters:

CALL GEORGE IN ATLANTA WITH JON IN LAS VEGAS
   WITH ME
RING ME WHEN READY
DISPLAY TELEPHONE IN BEDROOM

The personal computer system responds in a similar dialogue so that Jack can easily understand.

When Jack wants to use his system, he has only to speak one word loudly—"COMPUTER!"—and the keyboard lights up with a green glow. The keyboard displays a typewriter keyboard, and the CRT displays the time and date. When Jack strikes the ENTER key, the keyboard goes blank except for red-glowing numeric keys. The CRT displays a numbered menu of eight choices for Jack to select from. This dialogue continues until Jack is finished, and the personal computer thanks him in a prerecorded female voice.

What the Personal Computer of 1984 Will Look Like

Jack's computer system may be beyond the year 1984. We write a second scenario of Julie Zowie's home-centered personal computer instead in order to show you what is currently possible in 1977. If the five characteristics of a technological advancement are accurate, then by 1984 Julie's system may exist in homes throughout the country.

Julie Zowie has a personal computer system installed in her home that is connected to a nationwide entertainment network called HI-TVIS. Through her home system and telephone lines, she enjoys the following activities:

1. TV programs: Julie selects any program offered by the network during the current week. She may choose to watch now or record the program for later. She is billed directly for this service.

2. Information: Julie selects information including headlines from a newspaper, a book or microfilm from a library, or the weather report.

3. Facsimile: Hard copies are obtained for news items of interest to Julie. She selects the comic strip from last Sunday's paper. She is billed directly to her bank account.

4. Computer-assisted instruction: Julie inserts a tape into her personal computer system. Pictures appear on the TV screen, and she is asked to study the display. After a brief interaction with the lecture portion of this CAI tape, Julie takes an exam. Her answers are stored for later transmission to the university where Julie is enrolled in an economics course.

5. Cashless transactions: Stores, rent, utility charges, and bills are paid through Julie's personal computer and its link to the national network.

6. Computer browsing: Shopping and reservations are possible because Julie's accounts are electronically billed to her bank. She selects a dress from her favorite boutique and requests it to be sent to her address.

7. Home security: Julie's personal computer controls her burglar and fire alarms, gas and electric meters, and kitchen appliances.

Whenever something fails to operate properly, the diagnostic program is run to determine the type of repair.

8. Bookkeeping: Julie purchased a bookkeeping tape for her home computer. This tape has a program on it that does her tax return, handles her household budget, and so forth. She bought it from Ambitious Arnold, the accountant.

Julie purchased her home-centered system because it was inexpensive, a status symbol, fun, and necessary. She saves energy, time, and worry by using her personalized system. Julie is like thousands of others living in 1984 who own a technological device that is recognized as a profitable product for the manufacturer, priced below the threshold perceived by Julie as being "expensive," and above the threshold of being significantly more useful than the old way of doing things.

Communications for the Curious

The two scenarios of the previous sections suggest several areas where computers tie in with other technology. Indeed, the long-range future of computing is tied to a convergence between current technology that is not computer-oriented and yet deals with information. These technologies are centered around the computer because of its ability to control data, but it remains in the future for these "outside" technologies to join together into a network of combined machines and people.

The HI-TVIS system enjoyed by Julie Zowie and the teleconferencing facilities in Jack Sharpe's sea farm are all forms of networking. These networks depend upon communications for their success. Thus, an understanding of communications will be necessary to life in the future.

Networking May Mean You

In the future, space satellites and fiber optics will increase the capacity of communications services. This increased capacity will lower the cost of communications and add fuel to the vicious circles of technology. The resulting increase in the dollar-volume market for telecommunications will force new machines and systems into everyday use in future society.

The economic implications are not obvious, but consider this. When the cost of audibly, visibly, and tactually communicating over a two-way television channel becomes cheaper than the cost of an airplane ticket, who will choose to take the time and bear the cost of flying? When

Brazil, Paris, and Los Angeles are equally accessible by two-way TV for pennies, who will write letters?

The notion that one person can communicate with another regardless of their locations on the surface of the earth is one thing, but the concept of extending this notion to include many others simultaneously is staggering. Suppose it were possible to talk to all of your relatives, regardless of their telephone numbers. Further, suppose that the cost of doing so were reduced to a few dollars. What will this ability do to family reunions?

The final and ultimate vision is to imagine the networking of people *and machines.* Nearly all incorrect phone calls in the U.S. are currently handled by a computer. What happens when we are unable to distinguish between a human and a machine at the other end of the telephone line?

The fact that planet earth is being reduced to one large global village by electronic means is a subject with profound implications. Rather than re-examine those implications here, we shall move on to learn about the terminology and concepts of telecommunications in order to be ready for the future.

Some New Slang

The rate at which two machines can communicate with one another is governed by a limitation called *bandwidth.* The bandwidth of a *channel* (communications medium) is a measure of the frequency with which the signal changes. In computer terms, this would be measured in bits per second, a unit sometimes referred to as a *Baud.* If a telephone line is used to carry a 110-Baud signal, then the receiver at the other end of the line must be able to read at 110 Baud. This is a common speed of slow devices which use 11 bits to encode each character. Thus, a speed of 110 Baud usually means that 10 characters are being transmitted per second.

A computer is connected to a communications line in various ways. A serial connection, for example, allows the computer to input or output a single bit at a time. A parallel connection is able to transmit and receive 8 or 11 bits simultaneously.

There are a variety of names given to hardware connections because of the variety of standard connections possible. The most common connection, proposed by the Electronic Industries Association (EIA), is called an RS-232C interface. Other standards include the "current-loop" mode and IEEE standard bus connection.

A personal computer can be made to transmit bits at a given rate of Bauds and over a given connection. They can also transmit *asynchronously* or *synchronously.* An asynchronous transmission is a data transfer that contains no timing information along with the data. As a result, the receiving computer must wait for each character of data. The waiting computer performs a test on the connection line to determine if the data character has arrived. If it has arrived, the computer ceases to wait and reads the character into its memory.

Synchronous transmission is a data transfer that contains timing information along with the bit-by-bit information flow. The receiving personal computer is usually programmed to accept synchronous data at a very high rate (9,600 Baud) and directly inputs the high-speed data into its main memory, often over a DMA (direct memory access) arrangement provided by extra hardware.

In either event, the exchange of information between computers separated from one another is most frequently performed via a common carrier (telephone company). The carrier will provide one of the following types of services:

1. Dial-up
2. Point-to-point
3. Dedicated on-line

The dial-up service is usually a simple telephone along with a modem and acoustic coupler, as suggested in Chap. 3 (Mr. J. and the Savings and Loan). The personal computer is supplied with a Bell 103 type *data set*, as it is called, so it can "answer" the ringing telephone. The data set is a simple electronic device equivalent to an answering service.

The modem, acoustic coupler, and data set arrangement converts each bit of information into a tone similar to the tone generated by a touch-tone telephone. The tones are transmitted at 300 Baud, say, and decoded into bits at the other end of the telephone line.

On many personal computers a DAA (direct access arrangement) device is connected to the telephone to provide automatic dial-up, allowing the personal computer to do its own telephone dialing and relieving people of the chore. It also allows your personal computer to run unattended so that you do not need to be around when telecommunications take place.

The point-to-point arrangement provides a dial-up type of line that is dedicated to a single purpose. The line is used only to communicate computer data; it is not shared as is the dial-up configuration. It is also common to use point-to-point for noise-free, error-free communications because it allows for higher speed transfers. Typical point-to-point lines are conditioned by echo and noise suppressors to provide 2400-Baud, 4800-Baud, 9600-Baud, or higher data transmission speeds. Obviously, the point-to-point connection is more expensive.

The dedicated telephone line is a link reserved for intercomputer communication. No dial-up takes place, and the user need not be concerned about modems, couplers, and the like. The cost of dedicated lines will prevent their use in all but the most important communications applications.

The telephone company provides the necessary devices for handling the three types of data communications. Once the signal is converted to sound, it may be transmitted by cable, satellite, microwave, or newer technology methods like fiber optics or laser beam. In every case, there is room for error, and it is the prevention, detection, and correction of transmission errors that concerns computer designers. Here is why.

Suppose a computer file is transmitted once a week at the rate of 10 MHz (megaHertz). At this rate, 10,000,000 bits per second are copied from the file and sent to another computer. Suppose, further, that the error rate in transmission is one bit in every million bits moved. This means a rate of 10^{-6}. How many errors can be anticipated in a 10-minute conversation between this computer and another computer?

Since there are 600 seconds in 10 minutes, 6,000,000,000 bits will be transmitted in every 10-minute conversation. Of these six billion bits, one in every million is in error. The message would thus contain an average of 6,000 errors!

Communications engineers have developed techniques for detecting errors, and, in many cases, for correcting them. One simple method of error detection is called the *check sum*. We used check sums in Chap. 4. In communications, we can use a variety of check sums.

The *even-parity check sum*—also called *LRC* (see glossary)—is a single bit that is set or cleared (1 or 0) in order to force a binary word to contain an even number of set bits. The *odd-parity check sum* does the same, only it forces the sum of set bits to be an odd number.

The parity check sums detect only an odd number of errors. Thus, if the binary word contained an incorrect bit, or three incorrect bits, or five errors, or the like, then the parity bit will indicate this error.

A CRC (cyclic redundancy check) sum is a sophisticated check sum used to detect and correct single-bit errors, most two-bit errors, and some three-bit errors. It does this by using many bits intermingled with the data bits to check the data bits and also to check the CRC bits themselves. In CRC, the checking bits also have checking bits.

When an error is detected, but not corrected, it is necessary to retransmit the data. In the present example, we would have to retransmit the entire 6 billion bits whenever an error occurred. To do so would take an additional 10 minutes for each retransmission.

The retransmission may also contain errors. In the extreme, it may be impossible to get correct data because every transmission contains at least one error. This obstacle can be overcome by blocking the data into shorter bursts of data. Each block will contain fewer errors, and retransmission will be required less often.

The basic concepts of communication by means of working computers is in its infancy. The one thing that is clearly understood, however, is that the future will depend heavily on communications and control. The new slang of tomorrow's computer user will include words from today's communications engineer's vocabulary. These words will be combined with the computer control words we have used throughout this book to form the vocabulary of the twenty-first century man and woman on the street.

We turn finally to a last form of reading entertainment: the personal computer of the distant future.

What the Personal Computer of 1994 Will Look Like

The personal computer of 1994 will be a node on a communications network spanning the world. Anyone in any country will be able to access books, programs, money, people, services, and entertainment from his personal computer.

The computers described in contemporary science fiction novels may be available to consumers. A machine that speaks and listens to a limited number of words is totally possible. A machine that can see through a TV camera is also possible. In short, the personal computer of 1994 will be as near to a robot as we can imagine (even though it will not be mobile or look human).

The fable at the beginning of this chapter describes a possible scenario for the 1994 personal computer. This window to the future is only one view. There are many other views that include such things as the bionic computer and electrogenetics. But, of course, mankind must answer moral questions before these ideas can be implemented.

The personal computer of the future will have profound effects upon society. We can imagine a global mind arising because of the unified societies which result from close communications.

In the year 1000, the mentality of nearly all of Western society was at the level of a "village mind." The villagers knew only of their village and their thoughts were much the same as those of every other inhabitant of the same place.

In succeeding centuries, a "national mind" came into being in various

Western societies. Nearly every citizen of that period was limited in his thinking because he thought like every other citizen in his own nation.

An age of scientific and geographical exploration opened the world to a greater awareness. We became less egocentric and began viewing the world as less than central to the universe. In fact a few people were able to get a glimpse of the global mind that we are on the verge of now.

Einstein, space travel, and vast communications networks are plunging society into a new era of the global mind. The typical citizen with a global mind views his world in terms of the whole earth. Thinking has become broad in a fantastic sense. A few are even exercising their global minds in search of a galactic mentality.

The personal computer of 1994 is limited only by the limitations of the global mind. Awareness of the earth as a spaceship and of each other as human beings will decide how personal computers will be used. And there is only one thing to limit us: our grasp of knowledge itself.

Only lack of knowledge and lack of an awareness of the usefulness of computers are barriers to anyone wanting a personal computer.

GLOSSARY

Absolute address   A number that is permanently assigned as the address of a storage location.

Access time   The time required to locate a storage location.

Accumulator   A register in which the result of an operation is formed.

ACK/NAK   A positive or negative response by a receiving terminal to indicate whether or not a block of data has been received correctly.

Acoustic coupler   A form of modem which sends and receives data as tones over a telephone line using a conventional telephone handset.

Address   A label, name, or number which designates a location where information is stored.

Algorithm   A prescribed set of well-defined rules or processes for the solution of a problem in a finite number of steps.

Alphanumeric   Pertaining to a character set that contains both letters and numerals, and usually other characters.

Argument   (1) A variable or constant which is given in the call of a subroutine as information to it. (2) A variable upon whose value the value of a function depends. (3) The known reference factor necessary to find an item in a table or array (that is, the index).

Arithmetic unit   The component of a computer where arithmetic and logical operations are performed.

ARQ   An error control technique in which the receiving station responds with a NAK character if a message is received in error. The NAK is interpreted by the sending station as an *automatic repeat request.*

Array   An arrangement of elements into one or more dimensions. A one-dimensional array is commonly called a *vector*; a two-dimensional array is called a *table* or a *matrix*.

ASCII   An abbreviation for *A*merican *S*tandard *C*ode for *I*nformation *I*nterchange.

ASR   A designation used to indicate the automatic send and receive capabilities of teletypes equipped with punched-tape equipment.

Assemble   To translate from a symbolic program to a binary program by substituting binary operation codes for symbolic operation codes and absolute or relocatable addresses for symbolic addresses.

Assembler   A program which translates symbolic op-codes into machine language and assigns memory locations for variables and constants.

Asynchronous transmission   A mode of transmission using start and stop bits to frame a character (hence, frequently called *start/stop transmission*). Although bits within a character occur at well-defined intervals, they are not as precisely timed as in synchronous transmission, and characters do not recur at any predictable interval.

Atom   The elementary building block of data structures. An atom corresponds to a record in a file and may contain one or more fields of data. Also called a *node*.

171

Audio response unit   A unit used in "voice answer back" applications and digitally controlled to produce syllable and word response to persons entering keyboard data.

Auto-indexing   A form of indexing by means of which, when addressed indirectly, the contents of a location are incremented by new contents in the same location, which is then used as the effective address of the current instruction.

Autopolling   Performing the polling function automatically to reduce the data communication tasks of the host computer. Autopolling can be performed by communication preprocessors, multiplexors, data concentrators, and the like.

Auto-restart   A capability of a computer to perform automatically the initialization functions necessary to resume operation following an equipment or power failure.

Auxiliary memory   Data storage other than main memory; for example, storage on magnetic tape or direct-access devices.

Auxiliary storage   Storage that supplements main memory, such as disk or tape.

Average   The statistical mean; the expected value.

Average search length   The expected number of comparisons needed to locate an item in a data structure.

Backtracking   The operation of scanning a list in reverse.

Backward pointer   A pointer which gives the location of an atom's predecessor.

Balanced sort   An external tape sort that sorts by merging tapes together, each with an equal number of strings.

Bandwidth   A measure of the ability of equipment or transmission links to pass a range of frequencies.

Base address   A given address from which an absolute address is derived by combination with a relative address, synonymous with address constant.

Batch processing   A mode of data processing which processes one job after another in some order.

Baud   The maximum rate of transmission of signal elements, usually equivalent to bits per second.

Baudot code   A specific code using five bits to represent a character.

BCD code   A specific code using six bits to represent a character based on the Binary Coded Decimal representation of the decimal digits 0 through 9.

Binary   Pertaining to the number system with a radix of 2.

Binary code   A code that makes use of only two distinct characters, 0 and 1.

Binary radix sort   A radix sort in which the sort radix is 2.

Binary search   This search method begins with the middle element of a list and discards half of it, then, repeats on the sublist until the matching key is found or continuation of the subdivision produces an empty list.

Binary search tree   A binary search accomplished by storing a list in a binary tree. The tree is ordered when constructed or when insertions are made to facilitate the search.

Binary tree   A tree in which each node has a maximum outdegree of 2.

Bit   Either zero or one. It is derived from binary digit.

Block   A set of consecutive machine words, characters, or digits handled as a unit, particularly with reference to I/O.

Block search   To accomplish a block search, determine the block the item might be in, then linearly search the block.

Bootstrap   A technique or device designed to bring a program into the computer from an input device.

BPS   *B*its *P*er *S*econd

Branch   A point in a routine where one of two or more choices is made under control of the routine.

Break   A communication circuit interruption, frequently used by the receiving terminal to interrupt the transmitting terminal.

Broadcast   The transmission of a message intended for all receiving terminals connected to the communication channel.

BROM   *B*ipolar *R*ead-*O*nly *M*emory, a read-only memory using large-scale integration (LSI) bipolar devices.

BSC   An IBM designation meaning *B*inary *S*ynchronous *C*ommunication and referring to a specific communications procedure using synchronous data transmission.

Bubble sort   A sort achieved by exchanging pairs of keys, beginning with the first pair and then successive pairs until the list is ordered. Also called *ripple sort.*

Buffer   A storage space used to store I/O data temporarily.

Buffered I/O   A method of overlapping I/O using two or more buffers.

Bug   A mistake in the design or implementation of a program resulting in erroneous results.

Byte   A group of binary digits usually operated upon as a unit.

Call   To transfer control to a specified routine.

Calling sequence   A specified set of instructions and data necessary to set up and call a given routine.

Cascade sort   An external tape sort that sorts by merging strings from all but one tape onto the remaining tape. Subsequent passes merge fewer tapes until one tape contains all items.

Central processing unit   The unit of a computing system that includes the circuits controlling the interpretation and execution of instructions; also the computer proper, excluding I/O and other peripheral devices.

Channel, communications   A facility for communicating information. Also called a *link, line, circuit, data path,* and the like.

Character   A single letter, numeral, or symbol used to represent information.

Character checking   The checking of each character done by examining the characters as a group or field.

Character template   A device used to shape an electron beam into an alphanumeric character for CRT display.

Circular list   A linked list in which the last element points to the first one. Also called *ring.*

Clear   To erase the contents of a storage location by replacing the contents, normally with zeros or spaces; to set to zero.

Clear to send   An EIA RS-232-C designation applied to a sense circuit used by a terminal or computer to detect that its modem is ready to send data.

Clock   A device for timing events. In data communications, a clock is required to control the timing of bits sent in a data stream and to control the timing of the sampling of bits received in a data stream.

Cluster   *See* Primary cluster, Secondary cluster.

Code   A specific relationship between a set of bit patterns and a set of characters.

Code level   The number of bits used to represent a character (for example, the five-bit Baudot code is a "five-level code").

Coding   To write instructions for a computer using symbols meaningful to the computer, or to an assembler, compiler, or other language processor.

Collision   An act that occurs when two or more keys hash to the same address.

Column-major order   A method of storing a two-dimensional array in which all elements in one column are placed before all elements in the next column. This method can also be used to store higher-dimensional arrays.

Command   A user order to a computer system, usually given through a keyboard.

Compaction   Packing of data structure to make room in memory.

Comparative sort   Sort by comparison of two or more keys.

Compatibility   The ability of an instruction or source language to be used on more than one computer.

Compile   To produce a binary-coded program from a program written in source (symbolic) language, by selecting appropriate subroutines from a subroutine library as directed by the instructions or other symbols of the source program. The linkage is supplied for combining the subroutines into a workable program, and the subroutine and linkage are translated into binary code.

Compiler   A program which translates statements and formulas written in a source language into a machine language program, for example, a FORTRAN compiler. It usually generates more than one machine instruction for each statement.

Complement, one's   To replace all 0 bits with 1 bits and vice versa.

Complement, two's   To form the one's complement and add 1.

Completeness check   A check which verifies that no fields are missing and that no part of the record has been skipped in sequence.

Concatenation   The joining together of two or more strings to form a new one.

Conditional assembly   Assembly of certain parts of a symbolic program only if certain conditions have been met.

Conditional skip   Depending upon whether a condition within the program is met, control may transfer to another point in the program.

Connected graph   A graph in which it is possible to get from one node to any other node along a sequence of edges. If the graph is directed, the direction of the edges may be disregarded.

Connection matrix   *See I*ncidence matrix.

Consistency check   A check for consistency means that two or more pieces of data are considered in relation to each other.

Console   Usually the external front side of a device where controls and indicators are available for manual operation of the device.

Contiguous data structure   *See S*equential data structure.

Control character   A character inserted into a data stream with the intent of signaling the receiving station to perform some function.

Control totals   Control totals can be taken on amount fields or quantity fields of like sizes, such as units, dozens, or cases. These totals are added algebraically.

Convert   (1) To change numerical data from one radix to another. (2) To transfer data from one recorded format to another.

Count   The successive increase or decrease of a cumulative total of the number of times an event occurs.

Counter   A register or storage location (variable) used to represent the number of occurrences of an operation (*see* Loop).

CPS   *C*haracters *P*er *S*econd.

CPU   *C*entral *P*rocessing *U*nit.

CRC   A method of error detection using *C*yclic *R*edundancy *C*heck character(s). A CRC character is generated at the transmitting terminal based on the contents of the message transmitted. A similar CRC generation is performed at the receiving terminal. If the two characters match, the message was probably received correctly.

Cross-footing checks   Cross-adding or subtracting two or more fields and zero-balancing the result against the original result. This is an effective control when total debits, total credits, and a balance-forward amount are maintained in each account; total debits and total credits can be cross-footed to prove that the difference equals the balance forward.

CRT   *C*athode *R*ay *T*ube used to display information.

Current location counter   A counter kept by an assembler to determine the address assigned to an instruction or constant being assembled.

Cursor   A position indicator frequently employed in a display on a video terminal to indicate a character to be corrected or a position in which data is to be entered.

Cycle   A path which starts and terminates at the same node.

Cycle time   The time it takes a computer to reference a word of memory.

Cyclic redundancy check   *See* CRC.

Cylinder   The tracks of a disk-storage device that can be accessed without repositioning the access mechanism.

Data   A general term used to denote any or all facts, numbers, letters and symbols. It connotes basic elements of information which can be processed or produced by a computer.

Data modem   A modulation/demodulation device that enables computers and terminals to communicate over telephone circuits.

Dataphone   An AT&T designation for a service which provides data communication over telephone facilities.

Data set   Another term for *modem*.

Data structure   The relationship between data items.

Date check   A date check is done primarily to ensure that the record date is acceptable.

DDD   An acronym for *Direct Distance Dialing*, the facility used for making long-distance telephone calls without the assistance of a telephone operator. DDD is frequently used to mean the switched telephone network.

Debug   To detect, locate, and correct mistakes in a program.

Delimiter   A character that separates, terminates, and organizes elements of a statement or program.

Demodulation   A process for deriving information from a modulated carrier.

Dense list   A list stored in contiguous locations. Also called *linear list, sequential list*.

Density   The ratio of the number of information bits to the total number of bits in a structure.

Deque   A double-ended queue. A deque allows insertions and deletions at both ends of a list.

Device flags   One-bit registers which record the current status of a device.

Digit   A character used to represent one of the nonnegative integers smaller than the radix, for example, in binary notation, either 0 or 1.

Digital computer   A device that operates on discrete data, performing sequences of arithmetic and logical operations on this data.

Digraph   *See* Directed graph.

Direct address   An address that specifies the location of an instruction.

Directed graph   A set of nodes and edges in which an initial and a terminal node determine the direction of the edge. An edge from node A to node B is not an edge from node B to node A.

Directory   A partition by software into several distinct files. A directory of these files is maintained on a device to locate the files.

Display register   An internal register in a CRT display terminal.

Distributive sort   A sort achieved by partitioning the list and then exchanging items until order exists between the partitioned sublists.

Division checking   Division is usually checked by multiplication. This is done by multiplying the quotient by the divisor, adding the remainder, and zero-balancing the result against the original dividend.

Dope vector   An atom of a linked list that describes the contents of subsequent atoms in the list.

Double precision   Pertaining to the use of two computer words to represent one number.

Doubly linked list   A linked list in which each atom contains two pointer fields: one points to the atom's successor, and the other to the atom's predecessor.

Dummy   Used as an adjective to indicate an artificial address, instruction, or record of information inserted solely to fulfill prescribed conditions, as in a "dummy" variable.

Dump   To copy the contents of all or part of memory, usually onto an external storage medium.

Duplex channel   A communication channel with the capability of simultaneous two-way communication; equivalent to full duplex.

Dynamic memory management system   A memory system that supplies variable-sized space depending upon the request.

EBCDIC code   A specific code using eight bits to represent a character. The acronym stands for *E*xtended *B*inary *C*oded *D*ecimal *I*nterchange *C*ode.

Echo check   An error control technique wherein the receiving terminal or computer returns the original message to the sender to verify that the message was received correctly.

Echo-plex   A communication procedure wherein characters keyboarded by the operator do not print directly on his printer but are sent to a computer which echoes the characters back for printing. This procedure, requiring full-duplex communication facilities, provides a form of error control by displaying to the operator an indication of the character received by the computer.

Edge   That which connects two nodes in a graph; it may or may not have direction.

Editor   *See* Symbolic editor.

Effective address   The address actually used in the execution of a computer instruction.

EIA   Electronic Industries Association.

Empty string   A string containing no characters (of length zero); also called a *null string*.

EOB   End *O*f *B*lock.

EOM   End *O*f *M*essage.

Error control   A plan, implemented by hardware, software, procedures, and so forth, to detect and correct errors in a data communications system.

Error transmission   A change in data resulting from the transmission process.

Execute   To carry out an instruction or run a program on the computer.

External fragmentation   Memory loss caused by checkerboarding.

External sort   A sort in which all or part of a list is stored on an auxiliary storage device.

External storage   A separate facility or device on which data usable by the computer is stored (such as paper tape, magnetic tape, or disk).

Fail soft   A method of system implementation designed to prevent the irretrievable loss of facilities or data in the event of a temporary outage of some portion of the system.

Field   A unit of information.

Field checking   Checks concerned with the contents of fields within records.

FIFO   First *I*n, First *O*ut queue discipline.

File   A collection of related records treated as a unit.

File structured device   A device such as disk or tape which contains records organized into files and accessible through file names found in a directory file. *See* Directory.

Filename   Alphanumeric characters used to identify a particular file.

Filename extension   A short appendage to the filename used to identify the type of data in the file, for example, BIN, signifying a binary program.

Filial set   A collection of sons descended from a particular node in a tree.

Firmware   That portion of control-memory hardware which can be tailored to create microprograms for a user-oriented instruction set.

Fixed point.   The position of the radix point of a number system is constant according to a predetermined convention.

Flag   A variable or register used to record the status of a program or device; in the latter case, also called a *device flag.*

Flip-flop   A device with two stable states.

Floating point   A number system in which the position of the radix point is indicated by one part of the number (the exponent) and another part represents the significant digits (the mantissa).

Flowchart   A graphical representation of the operations required to carry out a data processing operation.

Forest   A collection of trees.

Format   The arrangement of data.

Forward pointer   A pointer that tells the location of the next item in a data structure.

Four-out-of-eight code   A communication code which facilitates error detection because four of the eight bits representing a character are always marking.

Fragmentation   Loss of usable memory caused by checkerboarding or mismatch in fit. *See* Internal fragmentation; External fragmentation.

Frequency   The rate of recurrence of some cyclic or repetitive event, such as the rate of repetition of a sine-wave electrical current, ususally expressed in cycles per second, or Hertz.

Frequency division multiplexing   The merging of several signals of lesser bandwidth into a composite signal for transmission over a communication channel of greater bandwidth. (Example: Five signals with a bandwidth of 100 Hz each might be accommodated on a channel having a bandwidth of 500 Hz.)

Full duplex   Describes a communications channel capable of simultaneous and independent transmission and reception.

Function subprogram   A subprogram which returns a single value result, usually in the accumulator.

Garbage collection   Release of unused portions of memory from a data structure to make unused areas of memory available for use.

Graph   A set containing two types of objects: nodes and edges. This provides a mathematical model for data structures in which the nodes correspond to data items and the edges to pointer fields.

Half duplex   Describes a communications channel capable of transmission and/or reception, but not both simultaneously.

Handshaking   A preliminary procedure performed by modems and/or terminals and computers to verify that communication has been established and can proceed.

Hardware   Physical equipment, for example, mechanical, electrical, or electronic devices.

Hash totals   A hash total is the sum of the digits of an identifying field.

Hashing   A key-to-address transformation in which the keys determine the location of the data.

Head   A special data item that points to the beginning of a list. A device that reads or writes data on a storage medium.

Header   The part of a message preceding the text, frequently specifying message destination, source, priority, etc.

Heap sort   *See* Tree sort.

Hexadecimal   A numbering system with 16 admissable combinations represented by the symbols 0 through 9 and A through F.

Hollerith code   A specific code using twelve levels of a punched card to represent a character.

Horizontal distribution   A method of assigning initial strings to tapes when employing the polyphase sort.

Huffman tree   A minimal value tree. *See* Minimal tree, Optimal merge tree.

Incidence matrix   A two-dimensional array which describes the edges in a graph; also called *connection matrix*.

Indegree   The number of directed edges which point to a node.

Index   A symbol or numeral which locates the position of an item in an array.

Indirect address   An address in a computer instruction which indicates a location where the address of the referenced operand is to be found.

Infix notation   A notation where operators are embedded within operands.

Initialize   To set counters, switches, and addresses to zero or other starting value at the beginning of, or at prescribed points in, a computer routine.

Instruction   A command which causes the computer or system to perform an operation. Usually one line of a program.

Intelligent terminal   A terminal with some level of programmable "intelligence" for performing preprocessing or postprocessing operations.

Interactive   A system which performs processing or problem-solving tasks by carrying on a dialog with the user.

Interface   A well-defined boundary, such as the interface between a modem and a terminal, or the interface between a communications controller and a computer's I/O bus.

Internal fragmentation   Memory loss due to mismatch between available space and requested size.

Internal sort   A sort made while all items remain in main memory.

Internal storage   The storage facilities forming an integral physical part of the computer and directly controlled by the computer; also called *main memory* and *core memory*.

Interpreter   A program that translates and executes source language statements at run-time.

I/O   Input/Output.

IRG   Inter-Record Gap.

Iteration   Repetition of a group of instructions.

Job   A unit of code which solves a problem, that is, a program and all its related subroutines and data.

Jump   A departure from the normal sequence of executing instructions in a computer.

K   An abbreviation for the prefix kilo, that is, 1024 decimal notation.

Key   One or more fields in a record that are used to locate the record or control its use.

Key to address   *See* Hashing.

KSR   A designation used to indicate the *K*eyboard *S*end and Printer *R*eceive capabilities of teletypes and comparable equipment.

Label   One or more characters used to identify a source language statement or line.

Language, assembly   The machine-oriented programming language used by an assembly system.

Language, computer   A systematic means of communicating instructions and information to the computer.

Language, machine   Information that can be directly processed by the computer, expressed in binary notation.

Language, source   A computer language in which programs are written and which require extensive translation in order to be executed by the computer.

Leaf   A terminal node of a tree.

Least significant digit   The right-most digit of a number.

Level   A measure of the distance from a node to the root of a tree.

Library routines   A collection of standard routines which can be incorporated into larger programs.

LIFO   *L*ast *I*n, *F*irst *O*ut stack discipline.

Limit check   A check that places upper or lower quantitative limits on a field

Line feed   The teletype operation which advances the paper by one line.

Line number   In source languages such as BASIC and FORTRAN, a number which begins a line of the source program for purposes of identification. A numeric label.

Linear list   *See* Dense list.

Linear search   A search that begins with the first element and then compares until a matching key is found or the end of the list is reached.

Link   (1) A one-bit register in most computers. (2) An address pointer to the next element of a list or the next record of a file.

Linkage   The code that connects two separately coded routines.

Linked list   A list in which each atom contains a pointer to the location of the next atom.

List   An ordered collection of atoms.

Literal   A symbol that defines itself.

Load   To place data or programs into internal storage.

Location   A place in storage or memory where a unit of data or an instruction may be stored.

Longitudinal redundancy check   A method of error detection using a parity bit for each level in the code being transmitted. Following a block of characters, an LRC character is inserted to make the number of bits transmitted on each of the code levels either odd or even. To check the accuracy of the received data, an LRC character is generated by the receiving terminal and compared with the LRC character received from the transmitting terminal.

Loop A sequence of instructions that is executed repeatedly until a terminal condition prevails.

LRC Longitudinal Redundancy Check.

Machine language programming This term is used to mean the actual binary machine instructions.

Macro instruction An instruction in a source language that is equivalent to a specified sequence of machine instructions.

Main memory The main high-speed storage of a computer in which binary data is represented by the switching of MOS transistors.

Manual input The entry of data by hand into a device at the time of processing.

Manual operation The processing of data in a system by direct manual techniques.

Mark The state of a communication channel corresponding to a binary one. The marking condition exists when current flows (hole in paper tape) on a current-loop channel, or when the voltage is more negative than -3 volts on an EIA RS-232-C channel.

Mask A bit pattern which selects those bits from a word of data which are to be used in some subsequent operation.

Masking A technique for sensing specific binary conditions and ignoring others. Typically accomplished by placing zeros in bit positions of no interest, and one s in bit positions to be sensed.

Mass storage Pertaining to a device such as disk or tape which stores large amounts of data readily accessible to the central processing unit.

Matrix A rectangular array of elements. Any table can be considered a matrix.

Memory (1) The alterable storage in a computer. (2) Pertaining to a device in which data can be stored and from which it can be retrieved.

Memory protection A method of preventing the contents of some part of main memory from being destroyed or altered.

Merge sort A sort which merges ordered sublists to form a larger, ordered list.

Message A group of characters communicated as a unit, typically including a HEADER, TEXT, ERROR CONTROL, and END-OF-MESSAGE indication.

Microprogram A series of microcommands assembled to perform a specific function.

Minimal tree A tree with terminal nodes so placed that the value of the tree is optimal. *See* Optimal merge tree.

Modem A modulation/demodulation device that enables computers and terminals to communicate over telephone circuits.

Modulation A process for impressing information on a carrier.

Monitor The master control program that observes, supervises, controls, or verifies the operation of a system.

Most significant digit   The left-most nonzero digit.

Multidrop circuit   A communication system configuration using a single channel or line to serve multiple terminals.

Multilinked list   A list in which each atom has two or more pointers.

Multiplex   In communications applications, the concurrent transmission of more than one information stream on a single channel.

Multiprocessing   Utilization of several computers or processors to divide jobs or processes, logically or functionally, and to execute them simultaneously.

Multiprogramming   Pertains to the execution of two or more programs in main memory at the same time. Execution switches between programs.

Nesting   (1) Including a program loop inside another loop. (2) Algebraic nesting, such as (A + B*(C + D)), where execution proceeds from the innermost to the outermost level.

Network   The interconnection of multiple communication channels and multiple terminals and /or computers.

Nil pointer   A pointer used to denote the end of a linked list.

Node   *See* Atom.

Noise   Signals bearing no desired information and frequently capable of introducing errors into the communication process.

NOP   An instruction that specifically does nothing (control proceeds to the next instruction in sequence).

Normalize   To adjust the exponent and mantissa of a floating-point number so that the mantissa appears in a prescribed format.

Null string   A string containing no characters; also called *empty string*.

Object program   The binary coded program which is the output after translation of a source language program.

Octal   Pertaining to the number system with a radix of eight.

Off-line   Pertaining to equipment or devices not under direct control of the computer or processes performed on such devices.

On-line   Pertaining to equipment or devices under direct control of the computer and to programs which respond directly and immediately to user commands.

Operand   (1) A quantity which is affected, manipulated, or operated upon. (2) The address, or symbolic name, portion of an assembly language instruction.

Operating system   A set of programs controlling the operation of a data processing system.

Operator   The symbol or code which indicates an action (or operation) to be performed.

Optimal merge tree   A tree representation of the order in which strings are to be merged so that a minimum number of move operations occurs.

OR, inclusive   A logical operation such that the result is true if either or both operands are true, and false if both operands are false.

OR, exclusive   A logical operation such that the result is true if either operand is true, and false if both operands ar either true or false. When neither case is specifically indicated, inclusive OR is assumed.

Origin   The absolute address of the beginning of a section of code.

Oscillating sort   An external tape sort which capitalizes on a tape drive's ability to read forward and backward. The sort oscillates between an internal sort and an external merge.

Outdegree   The number of directed edges leaving a node.

Output   Information transferred from the internal storage of a computer to output devices or external storage.

Overflow   An act that occurs if the allotted memory for a data structure is exceeded.

Pad character   A character inserted to fill a blank time slot in synchronous transmission or inserted to fulfill a character-count requirement in transmissions of fixed block lengths.

Page   A section of main memory.

Parallel transmission   The simultaneous transmission of all bits comprising a single character.

Parity   A method of error detection using an extra bit to make the total number of marking bits in a character either odd or even. If a character is sent with odd parity, it should be received with odd parity if no errors are introduced by the communication process.

Parity check   The examination of a character and its parity bit to determine if the character has been received correctly.

Parsing   The process of separating statements into syntactic units.

Pass   One complete cycle during which a body of data is processed. An assembler usually requires two passes during which a source program is translated into binary code.

Patch   To modify a routine in a rough or expedient way.

Path   A path from node n_i to node n_j: a set of nodes n_i, n_{i+1}, ..., n_{j-1}, n_j and edges such that there is an edge between successive pairs of nodes.

Peripheral equipment   In a data processing system, any unit of equipment distinct from the central processing unit which may provide the system with outside storage or cummunication.

Pointer   An address or other indication of location.

Pointer address   Address of a memory location containing the actual (effective) address of desired data.

Polling   The regular and systematic interrogation of terminals to determine if a terminal has messages awaiting transmission and to determine the state of readiness of a terminal to accept messages.

Polyphase sort   An external tape sort which works best with six or fewer tapes. A Fibonacci sequence of merges is established that maintains a maximum number of active tapes throughout the sort.

Pop   The act of removing an element from a stack; also called *pull*.

Postfix notation   A notation in which operators follow the operands that they operate on.

Primary cluster   A buildup of table entries around a single table location.

Priority interrupt   An interrupt which is given preference over other interrupts within the system.

Procedure   The course of action taken for the solution of a problem. *See also* Algorithm.

Program   The complete sequence of instructions and routines necessary to solve a problem.

PROM   Programmable Read-Only Memory. A semiconductor diode array which is programmed by fusing or burning out diode junctions.

Protocol   A set of procedures or conventions used routinely between equipment such as terminals and computers.

Pseudo-operation   An instruction to the assembler; an operation code that is not part of the computer's hardware command repertoire.

Pull   *See* Pop.

Push   The act of placing an element on a stack; also called *put.*

Pushdown list   A list that is constructed and maintained so that the next item to be retrieved is the item most recently stored in the list.

Put   *See* Push.

Quadratic quotient search   A hashing algorithm that uses a quadratic offset when probing subsequent table locations.

Queue   A list that allows insertion of atoms at one end and deletion of atoms at the opposite end.

Queuing   A method of controlling the sequence in which information is processed.

Quickersort   A sort achieved by partitioning a list into two sublists and a pivotal middle element. All items greater than the pivot go in one sublist and all lesser items go in the other sublist. Sublists are further subdivided until all items are ordered.

Radix   The base of a number system; the number of digit symbols required by a number system.

Radix sort   A distributive sort that uses a number of partitions equal to the sort radix.

Random access   A method of retrieving data from a secondary storage device in which the retrieval time is independent of the location of the data. Contrast with Sequential access.

Range check   A check that is usually applied to a code in order to verify that it falls within a given set of characters or numbers.

Read   To transfer information from an input device to memory.

Real-time   Pertaining to computation performed while the related physical process is taking place so that results of the computation can be used in guiding the physical process.

Reasonableness check   A reasonableness check is a programmed judgment on data to determine whether it is normal.

Record   A collection of related data items. A collection of related records make up a file.

Recursion   A reactivation of an active process; for example, a program segment which calls itself.

Recursive subroutine   A subroutine capable of calling itself.

Redundancy   A repetition of information, or the insertion of information which is not new and therefore redundant. Example: the use of check bits and check characters in data communication is a form of redundancy;

hence the terms: cyclic redundancy, longitudinal redundancy, vertical redundancy.

Redundancy check   The use of redundancy to check errors. *See* CRC, LRC, VRC.

Register   A device capable of storing a specified amount of data usually one word.

Relative address   The number that specifies the difference between the actual address and a base address.

Relocatable   Used to describe a routine whose instructions are written so that they can be located and executed in different parts of main memory.

Remote   Physically distant from a local computer, terminal, multiplexor, etc.

Replacement-selection   A tournament method of sorting tape files that produces ordered strings of various lengths which must be merged.

Response time   Time between initiating an operation from a remote terminal and obtaining the result. Includes transmission time to and from the computer, processing time, and access time for files employed.

Restart   To resume execution of a program.

Ring   *See* Circular list.

Ripple sort   *See* Bubble sort.

RJE   An IBM designation meaning Remote Job Entry and referring to the programs used to submit processing jobs from terminals.

RO   A designation used to indicate the Receive Only capabilities of teletypes and other equipment lacking keyboards and paper-tape equipment.

ROM   A Read Only Memory system wherein the stored bit patterns cannot be rewritten or otherwise altered.

Root   The node with indegree zero.

Routine   A set of instructions arranged in proper sequence to cause the computer to perform a desired task. A program or subprogram.

Row-major order   A method of storing a two-dimensional array in which all elements in one row are placed before all elements in the next row. *See* Column-major order.

RS-232   A technical specification published by the Electronic Industries Association establishing the interface requirements between modems and terminals or computers.

Run   A single, continuous execution of a program.

Scan   An algorithmic procedure for visiting or listing each node of a data structure.

Scatter storage   *See* Hashing.

Secondary cluster   A buildup along a path established by a pattern in a hashing function used for table look-up.

Segment   (1) That part of a long program which may be resident in main memory at any one time. (2) To divide a program into two or more segments or to store part of a routine on an external storage device to be brought into main memory as needed.

Selection sort   A sort achieved by selecting the extreme value (largest or smallest) in the list, exchanging it with the last value in the list and repeating with a shorter list.

Self-checking number   A self-checking number is one that has a precalculated digit appended to the basic number for the purpose of catching keypunch or transmission errors.

Sequence check   A check that is performed if incoming data records must be sequenced for further processing. If applicable, this type of check can be expanded to include a check on multiple records making up one transaction.

Sequential access   An access method for storing or retrieving data items which are located in a continuous manner. The retrieval time of an item depends in part on how many items precede it.

Sequential data structure   A data structure in which each atom is immediately adjacent to the next atom; also called *contiguous data structure.*

Sequential list   *See* Dense list.

Sequential search   *See* Linear search.

Serial access   Pertaining to the sequential or consecutive transmission of data to or from memory, as with paper tape; contrast with Random access.

Serial transmission   The transmission of the bits of a character in sequence, one at a time.

Shift   A movement of bits to the left or right frequently performed in the accumulator.

Simplex   Communication in only one direction.

Simulate   To represent the function of a device, system, or program with another device, system, or program.

Single step   Operation of a computer in such a manner that only one instruction is executed each time the computer is started.

Software   The collection of programs and routines associated with a computer.

Sort   The process of placing a list in order. *See* Binary radix sort, Bubble sort, Comparative sort, Distributive sort, External sort, Internal sort, Merge sort, Quickersort, Radix sort, Selection sort, Tree sort.

Sort effort   The number of comparisons or moves needed to order an unordered list.

Source language   *See* Language, source.

Source program   A computer program written in a source language.

Space   The state of a communication channel corresponding to a binary zero. The spacing condition exists when no current flows (no hole in paper tape) on a current-loop channel, or when the voltage is more positive than +3 volts on an EIA RS-232-C channel.

Spanning tree   A subgraph of a graph with two properties; first, it is a tree, and second, it contains all the nodes of the original graph.

Sparse array   An array in which most of the entries have a value of zero.

Stack   A list that restricts insertions and deletions to one end.

Start bit   A bit used in asynchronous transmission to precede the first bit of a character transmitted serially, signalling the start of the character.

Statement   An expression or instruction in source language.

Stop bit   A bit (or bits) used in asynchronous transmission to signal the end of a character transmitted serially, and representing the quiescent state in which the line will remain until the next character begins.

Stop code   A control character which, in the case of a teletype, turns off the paper tape reader.

Storage allocation The assignment of blocks of data and instructions to specified blocks of storage.

Storage capacity The amount of data that can be contained in a storage device.

Storage device A device in which data can be entered, retained, and retrieved.

Store To enter data into a storage device.

String A series of characters stored in a contiguous area in memory.

Structure The organization or arrangement of the parts of an entity.

Subroutine, closed A subroutine not stored in the main part of a program; such a subroutine is normally called or entered with a branch instruction, and provision is made to return control to the main routine at the end of the subroutine.

Subroutine, open A subroutine that must be relocated and inserted into a routine at each place it is used.

Subscript One of a set of characters used to index the location of an item in an array.

Swapping In a time-sharing environment, the action of either temporarily bringing a user program into main memory or storing it in a system device.

Switch A device or programming technique for making selections.

Symbol table A table in which symbols and their values are recorded.

Symbolic address A set of characters used to specify a memory location within a program.

Symbolic editor A system program which helps users in the preparation and modification of source language program by adding, changing, or deleting lines of text.

Sync character A character transmitted to establish character synchronization in synchronous communication. When the receiving station recognizes the sync character, the receiving station is said to be synchronized with the transmitting station, and communication can begin.

Synchronous transmission A mode of transmission using that synchronizes a character stream with a time bit stream.

Synonym Two or more keys that produce the same table address when hashed.

System A combination of software and hardware which performs specific processing operations.

Table A collection of data stored for ease of reference, generally as an array.

Tail A special data item that locates the end of a list.

Tariff A published schedule of regulated charges for common carrier services and equipment.

Teleprinter An automatic printing device operated by electrically coded signals from a keyboard.

Teleprocessing system Data processing equipment used in combination with terminal equipment and communication facilities.

Teletype Any of several configurations of keyboards, printers, and paper-tape equipment manufactured by the Teletype Corporation.

Telpak A type of communication link provided by common carriers; it represents a band of frequencies which can be subdivided into voice and data channels of various bandwidths.

Temporary storage   Storage locations reserved for immediate results.

Terminal   A peripheral device in a system through which data can enter or leave the computer.

Terminal node   A node of a tree which has no successors.

Test for alphabetic   This check guarantees correct alphabetic input.

Test for blanks   An indication must be made as to which fields must be blank. If the field requires blanks, a constant of the proper number of blanks is compared against the field, and a test made for an equal condition. An unequal comparison indicates an error condition.

Test for numeric   A numeric field is tested to ensure against having interspersed blanks and/or extraneous zone bits. Blanks are replaced by zeros. If the numeric field may not contain zone bits, zones are stripped from the field by the appropriate instructions.

Test for sign   This type of check is made to ensure that the proper algebraic sign is present for the type of transaction involved.

Text editor   A program that assists in the preparation of text.

Threaded tree   A tree containing additional pointers to assist in the scan of the tree.

Time division multiplexing   The merging of several bit streams of lower bit rates into a composite signal for transmission over a communication channel of higher bit-rate capacity. Example: five bit streams operating at 100 bps might be accommodated on a channel having a capacity of 500 bps. Combining the data streams is accomplished by assigning a "time-slice" of the high-speed channel to each of the low-speed channels.

Time quantum   In time-sharing, a unit of time allotted to each user by the monitor.

Time-sharing   A method of allocating central processor time and other computer resources to multiple users so that the computer, in effect, processes a number of programs apparently simultaneously.

Toggle   To use switches to enter data into the computer memory.

Token   A code or symbol representing a name or entity in a programming language.

Track   The portion of a magnetic storage medium which passes under a positioned read/write head.

Traffic intensity   The ratio of insertion rate to the deletion rate of a queue.

Transducer   A device that converts information in one form into information in another form.

Translate   To convert from one language to another.

Tree   A connected graph with no cycles. A directed tree is a directed graph that contains no cycles and no alternate paths. A directed tree has a unique node (the root) whose successor set consists of all the other nodes.

Tree sort   A sort achieved by exchanging items treated as nodes of a tree. When an item reaches the root node, it is exchanged with the lowest leaf node. Also called *heap sort*.

Truncation   The reduction of precision by dropping one or more of the least significant digits; for example, 3.141592 truncated to four decimal digits is 3.141.

Unattended operation   Transmission and/or reception without an operator.

Underflow   An act that occurs when an attempt is made to access an item in a data structure that contains no items. Contrast with Overflow.

Update   A method to modify a master file with current information, according to a specified procedure.

USASCII   An abbreviation for *U*nited *S*tates of *A*merica *S*tandard *C*ode for *I*nformation *I*nterchange, a specific code using seven bits to represent a character.

User   Programmer or operator of a computer.

Variable   A symbol whose value changes during execution of a program.

Vector   In computer science, a data structure that permits the location of any item by the use of a single index or subscript. Contrast with a table, or matrix, which requires two subscripts to uniquely locate an item.

Voice-grade channel.   Typically, a telephone circuit normally used for speech communication and accommodating frequencies from 300 to 3,000 Hz.

VRC   Vertical Redundancy Check. *See* Parity.

White noise   Noise (electrical or acoustical) whose energy spectrum is uniformly distributed across all frequencies within a band of interest.

Wideband channel   A communication channel having a bandwidth greater than that of a voice-grade line, and usually some multiple of the bandwidth of a voice-grade line.

Word   A unit of data which may be stored in one addressable location.

WPM   Words Per Minute, a measure of transmission speed.

Wrap data   The transmission of data through a communications system and the return of the data to its source to test the accuracy of the system.

Write   To transfer information from main memory to a peripheral device or to auxiliary storage.

INDEX